Table of Contents

MW01173014

Volume 3: Encyclopedia for Advanced Christian Learner, by Footage, Footprint, Calligraphy, and Carrier. 83

Volume 4: Arrival of Galaxy of Autobot, the Mighty God had visit us, the Thy Kingdom has begun. 145

Glossary 171

Croyalflush Ministry Foundation, Since 2011'活石事工基金会, 始于二零一一年.

The Legacy Christian Education & Reinvented Theology merge with Experimental Applied Physics & Proprietary Economics Science Ministry established Platform for Intellects & Computer Nerds.

The Legacy Christian Education & Reinvented Biblical Genetic Science, the Main Branch of Psycho Science, equipping you to end a Christian Journey.

A Scientific & Mathematical Approach to proof End time, Heaven, and Christianity. Not the least, a Biblical Approach to proof End time, Heaven, and Christianity.

独创的基督徒教育与重译神学结合实验应用物理学与专利经济科学事工创立完平台给知识份子与电脑愣子。

独创的基督教育结合重译圣经基因科学，精神病狂学的主要分支。装备你走完基督徒的道路。

用科学与数学的方法证明末世，天堂与基督教。更不止，用圣经的方法证明末世，天堂与基督教。

Those content in these website belong to Oversea Chinese (Guangxi) Medicine & Mandarin (Hainan) Theology Research Topics. Those Production, Reinvent, Publish or Abuse shall bear the Certain Responsibility or Consequences.

此乃华侨民族(广西)与大华民族(海南)的医学神学文案，如有雷同必追究到底。篡改者承当应当责任。

All original content on these pages is fingerprinted and certified by Digiprove.

Choose according to your Christian Equipped Learning Programs. 依照学习编程选择你的基督徒装备程序。

Medicine Renaissance 医药复兴, Biblical Genetic Science, the Biblical Approach to Learn Christianity 用圣经的方法学习基督教。

*Anglican i.e. Methodist by John Wesley is equivalent to reformed version of Catholic i.e. Vatican. a.k.a. Evangelical Methodist by Charles Wesley. Alpha to Omega, A to Z. Tree of Life. *Biblical Genetic Science is Medicine, oppose to Biomedical.

Vatican 梵蒂冈 (Post-Buddhism 佛教以后)

Buddhism i.e. Christian Music as Foundation; Santa vs Zombie

Economy Renaissance 高速经济, Economics Science, the Scientific Approach to Learn Christianity 用科学的方法学习基督教。

*Fundamentalism i.e. Presbyterian by John Calvin is equivalent to retro version of Eastern Orthodox Christianity. Alpha vs Omega. A to A'. Promised Land. *Christian Science is Pseudo Science, oppose to Applied Physics.

Ministry Foundation 事工基金会 (Post-Islam 回教以后）

Islam i.e. Christian Science as Foundation; Wizard versus Alien

Industrial Revolution 工业革命, Applied Physics, the Coding Approach to Learn Christianity 用编码的方法学习基督教 。

*Pentecostal i.e. Baptist by Martin Luther is equivalent to evangelised version of Lutheran. a.k.a. Charismatic by Martin Luther King. Alpha & Omega. Z to A. Eden Garden. *Coding Approach a.k.a. Engineering & Word Science & Artistic i.e. Linguistic Code. *Christian Mathematic is Pyscho Science, oppose to Psychology.

Witnessed Testimonial Event 见证分享会 (Post-Hinduism 印度教以后)

Hinduism i.e. Christian Mathematics as Foundation Christ vs Satan

Reading Policy 阅读政策

Reading Policy (i.e. The Information Contract Acts)

Devotion to Croyalflush Ministry Foundation: Instead of Charity, we consider our self as Functional & Solution Oriented Organisation exclusively to served God Ministry in terms, a. Christian Commission (Hymn Music Dominance, Information Management), b. Visionary (Christian Education, Technology Discovery), c. Missionary (Economy Miracles, Economy Science Breakthrough), d. Milestone (Theology Reinvention, Crime Disruption Objective). Hence, we are not accepting any Devotion in terms of Monetary forms, instead of that, Courtesy if those Legacy devotion via Author's Church Fellow & Islam Neighbour, Family's Connection, Alumni & Profession Union, Nationalist Network are appreciated. Those Legacy has growth into Copyright as time goes by.

Copyright: U.S. Copyright Registration Number: TX0009184097, 2022-07-17 &
TX0009107799, 2022-04-02 & TX0009116908, 2022-01-21, (United States Government Issue), Right and Permission under Claimant LAI Hin Wai. Purchase the Paid Content for free reading, and that is Public Property. According to Information Contract Acts. Those content in these website belong to Scientific & Theology Research Topics. Those Production, Reinvent, Publish or Abuse shall bear the Certain Responsibility or Consequences. The Copyright is certified and belong to Author, non-permit Transfer & Sell beyond Author Family, to achieve for high level confidentiality. The Copyright owner has the alteration and destruction rights, but same time bear the Full Responsibility or Consequences if infringe Law. Alternative, to deny Responsibility Bill is to convert the Copyright to Trademark or Patent or Service Mark, or Mental Abduction Burden.

Legacy: For Legacy donation you may approach the Secretary at hwlai@hotmail.com.
The Legacy contain Intellectual Property Assets and own it at condition of Fully Redemption of Undisclosed Missions or Contracts else Frozen Assets. Alternative, to
deny Obligation of Missions or Contracts Tax is to transfer the Legacy, or Jail Terrorism Burden.

Declaration: Croyalflush Ministry Foundation and Founder doesn't involve any
monetary activities such as Security Investing or Land Property nor any Intellectual

Property Copyright Selling except the e-commerce store. We don't written support but ignoring any kind of activities involving Terrorism, Mafia, Organised Conspiracy, Cold War, World War.

Manifest: Our Reinvented Applied Physics & Christian Education Solution focus on Resolution & Regeneration Information Management, & World Threat, especially Climate Change, Nuclear Ransom, Virus Variant Funding, Conspiracy Terrorism. In Addition, our Proprietary Economic Science & Theology Research focus on Decryption & Reformation of World Economics Miracles, & Economy Conspiracy hiding in Digital Economy, Clean Energy Economy, Rare Earth Economy, Knowledge Economy, Infrastructure Economy.

Finance Sponsorship: Gift owe to those Reputable Audit Profession i.e. Green Cards, Red Cards, Information Platforms, Ethical Property owner with Active Users Formally Compliment in this Ministry.

Last Update 8July2022, Croyalflush Ministry Founders

Topics Introduction 题材介绍

Volume 1: Oriental or Western

Chris Oriental Focus
War Insight: Weapon Methodology to Quantum Treasure
Criminology: Biblical Sins
Ending of Biblical Villain: Biblical Sinner Penalty

Volume 2: The Fringes of Final Inter-World Competes.

Clergy or Technie
Jesuit Economy Treasure Focus
Christian Politics: Social Science
Christian Medicine: Genealogy Technology
Classification of Ethnic: Ethnic Labelling & Graded
Politics Evolution: Series to Economic Harvest Reinvention

Volume 3: Encyclopedia for Advanced Christian Learner, by Footage, Footprint, Calligraphy, and Carrier.

Newbies or Dead End
Messi God Kingdom Focus
Social Engineering: Social Scamming
Christian Finance: Economic Methodology to Quantum Treasure
Biblical Application: Doctrinal Training
Christian Education: Theology
Puritan Music: Church Music

Volume 4: Arrival of Galaxy of Autobot, the Mighty God had visit us, the Thy Kingdom has begun.

Man Made or God Made
James New Nativity Focus
Christian Mathematics: Technology
War Insight: Weapon Methodology to Quantum Treasure
Hybrid Engineering: Military Technology

Preface 序言

About the Rainbow Bridge of Lost & Found Sheep, and Repel Lamb

Disclaimer: Independent Production, reinvent, disclosure, reproduction not granted.

承诺：独立制作，重译，转载，翻录必究.

- About Light Encyclopedia & End World Backup Plan 关于光百科与末世备份计划

Abstract: An Analysis from the point of view of Ethnicity, Technology, Religion and Economic. Guidelines escape to heaven.

摘要：从种族，科技，宗教与经济观点。逃离上天堂手册。

A long time since early days the prophecy civilisation of technology, music, religion as well as economic had reached out skirt of sky but without leaving clear records or demonstration to integrated what happening insight. Further, those histories After Christ Calendar was in muted, nothing can trace back what filled up the blank until the risen of United Kingdom 'Buckingham Palace' and Islam. These make a perfect description of what this book all about and rule out the future map of breakthrough.

On major side, the motive to write this book, named as [Light Encyclopedia & End World Backup Plan] , come from the point of view of Crime Key Person Disruption for Climate Change Conspiracy. Progressively, Human Right for Christian Persecution, Peace Union for War Crime, Church Reforming for Social Disorder, and Advanced Theology Application in Real World Issue for Technology Evolution as well as Economic Transformation, not the least, the concerning about the Crime Syndicate and Personal Security, there are Speed Evangelism, Explore Denomination Conflicts, Quran Verification for Religion Unity, Spiritual Equipping for Cult.

Last, accommodate for Advanced Civilisation, there are Authentic Pharmacy to New Age Medicine, Advanced Rocket Science Topics to Pseudo Science reinventing, Food and Music Demography to Humanity Heritage.

These are the reasons summary my intention bringing the good news from high and low to you and your family. I trust, in [Light Encyclopedia & End World Backup Plan] you may find peace, fruitful guidance, for the big uphold of the Lord and all his authentic disciples, to your great way for devout contribution to the kingdom in sky, the Praised 'Promised Land'.

Thanks.

序言

从较早前已有一段长时间，就预示中人类文明附属的科技、音乐、宗教以及经济已可到达天方之外，可却没留下明确的记录或指引对所发生的事情与内幕作总整合。 此外，所谓的基督后日历的记录是在全静音状态，没有任何事情可以追溯与填补空白，直至英国'白金汉宫'和伊斯兰教的兴起。 这些是对这是一本什么样的书的完美诠释，并概括未来蓝图的创举。

言归正传，写这本书的动机，即取名为 [光百科与末世备份计划]，是来自于对犯罪关键人物的瓦解与气候变迁阴谋。接着下去，人权与基督教徒的迫害、和平同盟会与战争罪行，教会归正与社会反秩序，高级神学应用与现实世界中的难题，衍生至科技的发展，经济转型。不只是这些，关注于犯罪组织和个人保安的，有迅速传道，宗派矛盾探索，可兰经考证至宗教合一，邪教属灵装备。

最后，预置高级文明的，有正统药剂至新世纪医学，高级火箭科学客题至伪科学重译，美食与音乐的人口分布至人文遗产。

这些理由概括我的意图，把好消息从高与低带到您和您的家人。 我相信，在[光百科与末世备份计划]里，您会找到和平、丰富果实的引导，为主和所有真实门徒，以虔诚的方式贡献于天空的王国，那被称颂的'应许之地'。

谢谢。

Croyalflush Ministry Founders
'Ryan' Lai Hin Wai, 'Richard' Lai Foo Ong, Thang Siew Kheng
11th August 2020

"I am the vine; you are the branches. If you remain in me and I in you, you will bear much fruit; apart from me you can do nothing. John 15:5

"我就是葡萄树，你们是枝条。那住在我里面、我也在他里面的，他才结出很多果子，因为没有我，你们什么也不能做。约翰福音 15:5

Acknowledgement 附言

First, thanks go to a lot of community, friends, fellows and business supported the binding of this book, including those important editors in Wikipedia.com, Youtube.com. Most importantly honour to my Lord, and my family & relatives, especially my mother Kheng and father Richard for continued and hopeless support. In addition, I have to thanks my affiliated church, JB Wesley Methodist, and Kindness Presbyterian, pastors Joshua and members of Church incl. Eagles & Ebenezer Cell Group devotion. I wish all the readers incl. my honourable Psychology Doctor Dr. Chan Teck Ming enjoy and support or join the Ministry of God.
Declares courtesy that any Legacy from Church Fellow & Islam Neighbour, Family's Connection, Alumni & Profession Union, Nationalist Network, and not the least I want to thank every Royals for any foresee accomplishment.

Thanks.

首先，感谢于那些社团，朋友，长老和业务对这本装订本的支援，包括那些重要的编辑 Wikipedia.com, Youtube.com. 最要紧的是荣耀我的主、我的家人和亲友，尤其是我的妈妈 Kheng 和爸爸 Richard 的不间断和不奢望的支持。我也要感谢我附属的教会循道宗卫理公会，与恩慈长老会，牧师 Joshua 和各小组与成员 e.g. Eagles, Ebenezer 的奉献。我希望所有的读者，包括我的荣誉心理医生，曾德明医生，的欣赏和支持或携起加入上帝的事工。

声明感谢任何商业机密来自于教会团契与回教邻居，家庭邦交，校友会与工程师联谊，联邦国网络，还不止这些，我还要谢谢各皇家对这本书后序的成全。

谢谢。

Best Regards,
'Ryan' Hin Wai, LAI
赖庆威
16th August 2020

Epilogue 后记

This is the second part of the series, including two sections. First, Oriental Blueprint, It meant the Heaven Decryption. The Know-how and Know-why of advancing the civilisation to next level in phase of environment, physical health and resource material.

Another section would bring you to witness what impact and highlights of Quantum Science Era transition Pentecost Science Era which is the 4G to 5G transition Era. Of course the highlights was within and in terms of Religion, Technology, Economics and Ethnicity.

Its an exciting fulfilment of all these efforts, indeed the Heaven Decryption Endervour, to push human civilisation, aligns with God will, to highest possible level and to auto pilot stage.

这是这系列第二部分，包括两个层面。一是东方蓝图，意为天启。在环境、身体健康和资源材料方面将文明推进到下一个阶段的技术与原理。

另一部分将带您见证量子科学时代转型五旬节科学时代的影响和亮点，即4G到5G的转型时代。当然，亮点是在宗教、技术、经济和种族方面。

这是激动人心的实现了这些努力，实际上是天堂解密运动，推动人类文明并符合上帝心意，以至达到可能的高峰和自动导航境界。
声明感谢任何商业机密来自于教会团契与回教邻居，家庭邦交，校友会与工程师联谊，联邦国网络，还不止这些，我还要谢谢各皇家对这本书后序的成全。

谢谢。

Best Regards,
'Ryan' Hin Wai, LAI
赖庆威
16th August 2020

Four Golden Book Conclusion 黄巾四步曲总结篇

The Christianity has break into Doctrinal (Root of Social Science), Theology (Root of
Natural Science) and Biblical (Root of Medicine), in which the Doctrinal is crucial cannot easily skipped, but unavoidable due to Denomination conflicts and Religion harmony.

E.g. Islam is the foundation in which Theology based, Buddhism is the Legacy which
inheritance to Biblical teaching, and Hinduism is the Fundamental in which the
Doctrinal based.

Yes, this is the final part, i.e. the conclusion part of this Series Trilogy Books. We had
illustrated the Ethnic & Politic, Computer & Social, Crime & Economy, Medicine &
Business and Science & Engineering are progressive inter-related since book 1, book 2 and book 3.

Book 1 is Evangelism from Heaven i.e. Catechism from Heaven, Book 2 is Adventist of Heaven i.e. Civilisation Breakthrough, and Book 3 this book is Guide to Heaven, i.e. Pentecostal to Heaven.

四步曲总结篇

基督教已经分为教规（社会科学的核心），神学（自然科学的核心）和圣经（医学的核心），其中教规至关重要，不能轻易跳过，但难免于宗派冲突与宗教和谐。

例如，伊斯兰教是基督教神学的基础，佛教是基督教圣经的传续，印度教是基督教教规的范畴。

是的，这是最后一部分，即系列三部曲书籍结论部分。我们已经清楚教导，即种族与政治，电脑与社会，犯罪与经济，医学与商业以及科学与工程，从第一本，第二本和第三本，第四本。这些内容是相互关联的。

第一本是从天堂传下福音 i.e. 圣经问答，第二本是天堂复临 i.e. 文明锐变，第三本，是天堂搬步，i.e. 五旬登天。第四本，是坠落拯救，i.e. 神学福音。

Volume 1: The 7th Heaven, the Capita Blueprint.

Oriental or Western

Chris Oriental Focus: From Utopia Beta to Utopia Final

Criminology: Biblical Sins
War Insight: Weapon Methodology to Quantum Treasure
Ending of Biblical Villain: Biblical Sinner Penalty

Y414. Is it the End of the World or Charismatic Church? (Forum)

When it comes to Spiritual, the first thing to ask is the Works of Spirit. Of course, Spiritual is for individual, but Works is for Public.

The interactive part in spiritual, reflect out the works. Hence, a mere mind change could cause a hurricane. If the atmospheric is right. Atmospheric just the frequency. Resonance happen at under same mode of factors.

So prayer could make great victory. You cant bluff. But now, Quantum weapon invented.
I don't know.. take your freed.

The tragedy in Korea meant alot to the Christianity. It tells Christian has to be Schism, than Connected.

Job Workaholic versus Flower Fever. The Schism of Christian make up the Dollar vs Pound. The Matter and Medium. Blue vs Hymn.

How could the Pentecostal Church Split? Just by Two kind of Pentecost. The Chromatic Light vs White Light. It split the Church into halves. The Blind Faith and True Faith.

No third. Its about Salvation by Condition and Salvation by Determined. And this could brew Third World War.

Some of the Church are the 3rd Kind bordered. In religion, it is about Black and White. Not Colour Boundary.

Those running on the steel wire is dangerous. To Korea Disaster, I would condemn the Christian Education did harm things.

It need recovery plan to retrieve the loss for all poisoned. The Now Comes Christmas 2022. Let's make a review and Great Leap.

There aren't enough to survive. Let change the World Axis point to the Right Datum.

Amen.

There are bad teaching.

Y438. The Begin Of Universe Begins With Star Dust Collector (Forum)

Impossible is impossible. Unless you make your own timeframe. Never jump conclusion. What you disagree, cost you. This is called terms and conditions and called the blind.

The Machine Generations of 14. And the Calculator generations of 12. e.g. From 3G, 3.5G to 8G. Precisely is Germanium, Calcium, Quart, Pearl, to Silicon Configuration.

For Chronography purpose. James Webb Telescope? And for Calligraphy pursuit, the current generations is Organic Fibre printer.

The Germanium and Pearl Land. Precisely is Silicon Valley. Interesting to know where Israel Elections comes from?

The 1st Demography Rich Country. In another the Military Regime. Hence, the Ukraine so on.

In which the oldest place of this world. Just from the Geneva time. In fact, the most advanced city in this world.

Blind hope does make sense. This is called Timed Demography of 30+1 sec. Forward Backward.

And the Bottleneck of this pin on Economy Loading. i.e. The Non-Christian Loading, and Christian Burden.

Which automatic count forward for those High Calibre as Christian ethnic. Precisely is those High Belt.

One Country has 2 Leader. One King and One Jack. First of all, camping effect must be corrected.

It has to be tie on the Heaven. It means the Duty and Levy make you perfect in regardless any situation. i.e. Atonement of Sins.

This proven the 3 Milestone of Quantum effect. In whatever situation, you won't be starved or dive.

As long your community remained as one whole body. Simply the Gun shooting point toward Genocide.

This is Surprisingly Reflected the Chronicle Community. The Disruption of Noah Act. This is from the Third World Conspiracy, put it in Jealous way.

The Kelvin temperature determine our Economy. And fortunately, it is automatic unless you rejected.

Those rejected of Food, are Anti God, a.k.a. Anti Semitic. So, the Root has two, but Destination has only one.

Those people heading to Renaissance Rome, are brew 'T', because of they are not the Election of Gods.

This make up the Six Sigma at 80% Percentile. Put it in another words, the 60% of World Population are In-mobility.

This just liked the Traffic Jam. When Road to Israel is Blocked, the Road to Oriental is Opened.

This Weighing effect could brew Tsunami. There is evidence that we are affected. This is the so called Fake News.

This is the Guarantee of Believer, to your Property Heritage your belonging and you remain as one. No Duty required.

The Street Protest has becoming popular now, as people use this to create their own Extra Time.

Their time has wasted into Fine Dining. When there is Marriage Misconduction, there must Censored from our eyes.

You won't find it, trust me. Those capture are the Lawful. This is the Solar Wave Warning if you disobey.

So, make up Max 20% Percentile of Any Genocide Population. It is impossible more than that risk.

Called Prime Guarantee. Those Elections of God. Of course, 20% is also meant the Max Grace.

So, there are people choose to it. And this is Rigid. People create Harps Effect, and people create War, no yield. And there is special group of Heaven inheritance, more than the God election groups.

Holistic Principle is a cards field. And this will fasten maturity to unity than delayed. So equipping with Holistic principle is the best bet.

This is the Gold Mining, with No Market Value. But bring up the Technology is the only way we can do.

Some work for other, some other work for you. One crab the space, strike the heaven heritage.

This is called Spiral Road. Each and every one of us goes up. 100% in Total Freedom. The backward are those goes beyond. Those create Anarchy. When Politic failed the Nation success.

Geometric Ranking Methodology. a.k.a. Lambda Ranking, 3 Step. Lambda Knot. Moses Correlation Code. e.g. Rockwell Method. Dialectic Method.

From geometric cryptography Meta Ranking, sufficient to plot out the Whole Global Map. And the 5 geometric configurations plot out the demography.

The Chronography determine the Geometric Axis. There are alot Calendar Method, and the most concise is the one plot out demography Axis.

This method can be used on Missile Shielding. The insight is on the Body Heat management.

Hence, this can be used on Flying Helicopter Shielding. The Algorithm is represented by a Configuration of Geometric.

The best way is represented by Series of Rhetoric. It can be used to move the Asteroid. And also Self Commuting. Newton first Law.

This is the reformation of both theory. There are 3 Newton Scaled. And this 3 Newton are in one, as liked in three. Where there is Newton IV, the time may freeze. And the Newton IV is the Anti Gravity.

When time freeze, the Gravity diminished. It is a special channel of those Newton IV community. When Demography maturity, it is the time.

Road Construction Code Determine the Spiritual Maturity. a.k.a. Kelvin Mark. It is mirror and mirror. Only 3 Boundary. Sea, Land, Sky.

This call also tells from Hall Mark, and Time Chronology, and Kelvin Lambda Knot. The shielding are using the Lambda-ray beam.

Using the Moses IV Code i.e. Newton IV. Translated to Quantum 8,10,7. The Moses Code Interaction Step, mean Quantum number the interative.

Hence from the Quantum number, we make determine the Chances of Strike. e.g. the 1st President and the Last President.

This is always Opposite. due to Linearity. The Next is final, as golden rule. No more. The Crab is the final.

So when it is the worst politic, it is the best nation. The Chronography is rotational datum on 2nd, and 8th and 13th.

This make Jewish, top 12 tribes, Celt 5 clock wise tribes and German 5 anti clock wise tribes.

Clock wise and anti clock wise mean the Newton I, II. It has pinned. When this 3 People comes together, it formed Newton IV. Its only 24 mile to make Tee.

24 milestone incl. the Clear 4 dragon stage. We have Six Sigma the Seal, and 4 Lambda the dragon.

The Esther Law cannot be Abuse. From this Statistical Technique, identification hard to be hidden. The Genetic morph become trial now.

The entire effort is spend on disruption of Newton I,II,III community. The white mice race fight.

So this is the danger zone of genetic morph. One word, Esther Law is seriously abused. and required international sea law control the High Voltage Electro Device.

And this is exactly the community genocide and social reverse engineering. The Spiritual Information bomb.

The Islam Kingdom and Extremist Christianity. Creating Christian James, or Islam Noah.

Entire effort away from Newton I,II,III become Unity. Hence, the Islam states is in Dubai Tower. Middle East and South East Asia Islam is Clock wise and Anti Clock wise, from the Beards.

The Obstacle of this, is strategical mistake of dilemma of Creating Brexit Economy. The Globalisation. And Asia advanced Western on Globalisation endeavour.

And form up series of iterative step to form up Republican Community, i.e. Newton I,II,III. 5 Continent each live 1 king and 1 jack.

Everything is plotted, what isnt is the 4 Lambda dragon, and 6 Sigma seal. And the Penta Computer Born. and Five Lens Camera born too soon.

To capture Newton IV beam. There are 14 generations of Newton Beam, but only 4 beams is Carrier.

The Cold Beam. Those God made, man cannot made. It is called Automatic. To group human is easy, to judge human is no way.

This is God made thing. The God making failure more failure. and Gentile more gentile. And you can only run.

Hence, rich become poor, and beauty become nun. Be the lame, you are protected. Quit the day, away the Newton VI. It is attached all thing on the G string.

The Puppy. Yes the New Human. The Backup plan become the Premium plan. When this happen, it mean Parallel.

The Dark Red Solar happen. The Supernova star born. This is habitat. In fact, this is the sole power of the whole universe.

It has alot of Oxygen. Some Christian like the Supernova, living in the Crowd City. and some like the Interstellar trip, living in the Twin City. And the Interstellar trip can make Newton IV, the Heritage booming.

The Weapon law make marriage misconduction more risky. Just to name a few. Business Misconduction as well as Marriage Misconduction is like crossing the mountain.

The Time Tax when end time make Everything more clean. When supernova form, the Universe reverse. The Romance Zone formed.

Those Renaissance place. Anti Semitic Place. Hence Renaissance mean Third World. Third World you cannot go, and couldnt go.

The reason insight is Zone Lock by Newton VI. The Lamb is the Primary source of Happiness. And to reverse all this just simply change the Road Construction Code also point toward the Road Block.

Immediate effect. The Spiritual Game is Forbidden, Seriously Abuse. This is not about Science Technology, but Spiritual Game.

It is real power. Very evil and blasphemy to God. Simply kit. Another belief is Time Shift by Solar Wave modification.

This can be reflection. When you seeing of this technological breakthrough, it is scamming.

The Bad Iconic. Good Rocket and Bad Rocket could bring Devil on stage. The little thing could make great disruption. playing dark magic make money, playing white magic costing and temporary.

Its loyalty and royalty. Not all renaissance same. differ by Meta clock. 4 directions. The insight is the Newton generations.

The dominated Newton generations. Jewish, Celt and Germans, and Israelite. Jewish the Aegean Culture.

The Germans, the Music Evolution. The Celt, the White Magic Press Technology. The Newton, Beethoven, Augusta. And the Israelite has no one since A.D. Hence, this is the forever rule.

Those belong to Third World just go. Let past be seal and go forward. Every day is a progress.

We will clear the stage. No matter how, this is just a joke. Good health most important, right.

Too bad, you cant have it all. I meant it sound to me. The ant has no help. Hall mark proven.

It got to call in. This is the strictest Esther Law. Tax is hard collected. It is not a donation. Do business like ancient you win.

Earth has become a Star Cube. Which part rotten is clear. The Call in required. It is the past, and as liked ancient.

Where the Geneva time correlated. Before Geneva Time, the World has no Star Cube. The Formed of Geneva time, it is the beginning of universe.

The New Universe. and this Universe is not belonged to Evil. Blind guess. There are no more Extra Terrestrial but become one part.

But time can squeeze. It is called Inter Space. For Star cube is Self-Resonance itself. So this become 6 axis and 6 mode.

The Weather mode. So, 6 axis vibration and rotation is liked. Star dance. This just like the Dog sniff.

It is a progression too. Progression and program are difference. This eventually turn out into two tips support.

Just like the Aircraft wheel. It is lower down. When that happen, the planet become into flying planet.

Steady one. And the whole universe follows too. It makes evil become locked. This required a little push from alien.

When the alien moves, it moves the world. This has no brake. And that only superman can do. When it hit another planet, that is super planet a.k.a. Supernova.

It is just like Supernova hit Black Hole yield one more timer, the Lap timer. The Geneva and Waterloo formed Top 7 Communities.

Insight, the Begin of Universe begins with Star Dust Collector. And, Posted with the Star Dust Payer. The heaven calls you. Ahh?

Y415. The Rootcause of Third World Country (Forum)

In UK, is "mind your own business". In US, is "all is my business". Who harvest? Its about Profit versus Revenue. Hence, Wealth can made, and Technology can made. American Focus on Sells, and British Focus on Delivery.

This break down Electronic Commerce into 2 sector. The Free Content Provider and Clean User Database. And Free Content Provider is Profitable, Clean User Database Client is Sustainable. This is why Online Enterprise close down but Online Marketplace sustain.

The reason is on Audience. Clean or Active. A Hybrid concept can make applicable into good use. But Fundamental thing no change. Alot different, if make hybrid to accommodating or communicate more users. This is the China University teaching. It could comes out a booming economic myth. But after all, Economic Myth is just volatile. Take note.

Its have had to sync with Harmony with Counter part, like a fish. The Duality of Ecommerce. Hybrid Engineering and Duality Commerce. One back one forth, a dilation of 40 years. The number of population accommodated is by 100% percentile, and 50% percentile.

How to translate, but Biblical sound logic. The Tolerance make African Right. The Tolerance make Islam religion right. Christianity is high demand religion. This is Racialism rootcause. This terms called Economic Loading.

Its about Zero Loading to High Loading. So any Economy Body Could created 100% Percentile of Accommodate. The Reason of Failure is due to Racialism. This is what God promised, the Eternal Life.

Its a Duality concept. So some people are too contented. What I mention before, the Economic myth is just volatile without connecting to God. That is Rome. All Road lead to Rome.

It can be understood as, something wrong with Racialism. We must have a Global acumen. Make 75% Percentile Right. There must a loophole of emergency but not publicized. The Express lane for making Billionaire is a closed gate.

This is about the datum of genetic. The Honey and Milk make the greatest. There Axis is on the Jew the Bottomline. This is about the Genetic as well as International Law.

The reason is not about the graded but pre-requisite the condition of salvation of all. The Jew Community is the largest community, and this make Economy Burden.

Take the best and make the bottomline. Top 25 percentile. These people has the best Trade Secret of all kind of Engineering. Those are called Man Made products.

The Robin and Cat women. Same thing apply to Nuclear Weapon. Nuclear weapon is a fusion technology, and this is required alot of Dead Soul.

It can only happen in third world. This is the Guarantee, only Racialism can make third world country. Those disagree with top 25 Percentile Jew, is Anti Semitic. Those country are not Poverty but alot of Disease.

THEY ARE RICH. But just volatile. Who moves my cheese...Good command of english determine Third World or Developed World. Computer Literacy is the gauge.

The resolution is to let both growth, multi-literalism. You will surprise that Fig tree has leaf. Each communities are growth at their own speed. The Computer literacy and Music immunity is gauge.

There is no hybrid communities, but back and forth. When it comes to Hygienic, the sensitive come first. Its destiny after all.

This is equivalent.

Y593. Criminology XXX: Suspected Terrorism Motive of Series (Census)

Hillary as the Caesar Queen issue Banknote the Hijacked Old Whitehouse (ISIS).
Recruit False Fasci UN team as Blacklist the Scapegoat (i.e. that point toward Malaysia-Singapore Chinese Dispute on Chinese Royalism and Chinese Democracy Global Treat Issue since **'64' Tiananmen**),

And same time Possess the Dictatorship of True Fasci UN team as Whitelist Scapegoat as Global Class Executive Agency, suspect Quantum Satellite Series Formation Climate Change the Kelvin Mark Mod Activities incl. 2020' **Covid-'19' China**.

ISIS Chief as Remastered Pentagon Membership
The Whitelist Scapegoat Activities incl. Series of Terrorism aftermath, since 2001 **'911' New York**, and until Covid-19 Quantum Weapon present now.

List of Ranks

#1. NeoNazi team member, True Fasci UN team – **False Eucharistic Church Licenses Executive Agency. (Pope, Ecumenical Judification Milestone) (Nazi Democrat NASA, Holy Spirit Scalar, ISIS Stakeholder, Hijacked Vatican)**
Universe Physics Constant as **Climate Geothermal Weapon**
Add on: Islam Pope (Devil), Unicorn (Satan), The Male Nazareth (False Christ)

#2. NeoNazi team member, True Fasci UN team – **False Royal Doctor as Queen Issued the Coherent Banknote. (God Father, Economic Summit Congress) (Fasci Socialist UN, Tither Modular, Fasci Whitelist)**
Christian Rating as **Biomedical Eye Viral Weapon**.
Add on: Zechariah (False Prophet), Unicorn II (Satan II), Chris (Christ)

#3. NeoNazi team member, True Fasci UN team – **False Computer Security Protocol. (Dalai Lama, Industrial & Medicine Framework) (Nazi Communist Zion, Legislation Chancellor, Fasci Mafia Dragon i.e. Security Bankruptcy Qing Organised)**
Quantum Sky as **Social Mind Weapon**. Add on: Herald Dalailama (Serpent), Herald Islam Pope (Serpent II), Royal Doctor of Global Class (Man of Sins)

A. Jihad Spiritual Prophet: *Devil (2nd, Tournament)*

Fasci NATO (Russian Underground Mafia), Misconduction of Church the "Turkey in the Straw" (The Transformer Machine became abandon from Christian to Islam, and no other equivalent Machine). The Chinese Security Bank Frauding & Politic Frauding Mastermind, and threaten to China incapability Governor 18 Scalar Team.
Biblical Villain, Stellar Head: Islam Pope (Devil)

B. Christ the Salvator: *False Christ (5th, Over Exposure)*
Fasci UN, Dalai Lama 18 Rohs, 101th (Alpha & Omega Olive Dust)
Biblical Villain, Stellar Head: The Male Nazareth (False Christ)

C. Story Teller Wolf Eat children: *Satan II (3rd, Remotely)*
Fasci UN, Democrat Chancellor (Qing Syndicate Organised Crime Security Prime Funding), Blacklist Scapegoat (Prime Person Hijacked Whitehouse, and Affiliation to Pentagon)
Biblical Villain, Stellar Head: Unicorn (Satan)

D. Titus the Islam Mafia: *Serpent (4th, Comfort Zone)*
Fasci Zion, Islam Jihad Prophet, ISIS Herald, Stellar Head
Biblical Villain, Stellar Head: Herald Islam Pope (Serpent II)

E. Prison Chancellor: *Man of Sins (1st, Last Resort)*
**Fasci NATO, ISIS Terrorism Training Camp the Royalist of Free),
Whitelist Scapegoat**, as Surgent the Bruteforce to Democracy Innocent.
Biblical Villain, Stellar Head: Royal Doctor of Global Class (Man of Sins)

F. Adventist Congress: *False Prophet (6th, Islam Company)*
Fasci Zion, (Nazi Organised Mafia), God Father, Blacklist Antichrist Think Tank, 99per (Best Ranked)
Biblical Villain, Stellar Head: Zechariah (False Prophet)
*Stellar Head a.k.a. Stellisation Head or Pyramid MIS.

Y520. War Insight XXVII: Etymology of MH370, Rootcause of Budget Airline (Whiteboard)

Conspiracy MH370 Revealed

Mafia DPRK from Taiwan to US
Mafia Korea from Malaysia to US
The 38 Lent: Universal Capita Regime Headquarter

The U.S. Jew Native vs U.S. Jew Diaspora
Oversea Chinese vs Traitor Chinese
The Medicine Framework Chinese Inaugural Bank

The Hijack of Whitehouse 1st, and replicating the same Profit by Hijack of Buckingham.

Energy Cost Exchange is Technical Capita Camp, for Bargain Power.
The IT streaming in Asia.
incl. Pilot Secretary vs Administrator, Framework Architect vs Manager, Coding Inventor vs Executive

Wage deficit Geographical, the Career Crisis happen in IT Downstream, the Technical.

The Rule out of Gross Capita Exchange **Regime** the **Nazi Headquarter** from Malaysia to Singapore, into the Remote Basement. And Malaysia point out as Christian Persecution the **Fasci Headquarter**, Gross Capita **Treasure** Deficit, the Primary Basement.

Hence, MH370 replicating dilemma determined the leap of Korea Religion Regime Ambition into Dynasty. The Mafia Organised, i.e. Nazi Pillar, World Bank, a.k.a. **ISIS Headquarter**. The Economic Congress.
The DPRK determined into Mafia Underground, i.e. Fasci Pillar, Security Bank a.k.a. **ISIS remote basement**, the Pentagon. The Semitic Congress.

Since the beginning, ending route or foresee vision, this has became the "Fusion Effect" and goes on replicating until the End of World fictionally.

Motive is to make Chaos to Covering Korea from Disaster Duty Ransom.

There has becoming the Erotic Exchange Basement for Military Defence Excuse.

The Air Mystery is the explain of Recovering of those Missing Identity & their Credential.

Thought the Timer Crisis untold, (related to the Duplication of this into Other Country).
e.g. Road Protocol by Road Barrier Scamming.

The Etymology of MH370 is 999 Lost and Found Sheep, 1% of Log, the Metric Scaled.

Hence, signifying the Semitic Congress Mileage to begins the Eschatology Calendar Journey.

This is a Status of Jewellery per Gross Capita.

The Famous Quote of Apollo, Neil Armstrong, "The Smallest Leap to the Biggest Step".

Y584. War Insight XXXVI: Last Blood the False Minor Prophet & Hostage Hiding (Whiteboard)

False Minor Prophets & Hostage Hiding

i. Malachi (Alternate Core Stakeholder, Devil/Man of Sins): Christmas Day, Santa Claus
Queen Made, Harbour Dust, Rib of Man the Carbon Dating and Carbon Imprint
Titus, Dramatic Love, Public Ministry (Cent the Blood, Fever), the Any – Any (Black Dragon Organised 卧龙,黑龙/Ancient Dragon Nazi Zion False Prophet 古龙,龙的传人) in Renaissance, the Express to Heaven. Fire Lake (Age Lock Full Mileage, Colony) Route
Alternated Core 16 (Commuting Gap the Interval, Same School the Long Journey) in 24 Heaven (Mafia Dynasty, toward Promised Land)
Nazi Zion, Western Security Bank in US AU (Iron Weapon)

*Hijacked the 2nd 911 Prevention (Epidermic Genocide) 民粹泛滥,草根兵团失败告终

Coherent Generations 堂氏 (Organic Made 土作)
Israelite 政要: African Ashed Skin (Orthogonal Three Date Required, Trinity-ism) vs Indian Inked Skin (Pentecost One Date Only, Monotheism)
Virginia the Antichrist: Due to Lent Burden on Humanity Crime as low as Misconduction of Marriage
Germanic 江湖 (Monotheism): Antichrist, Prime Inked Skin Those Under-Cultivated

ii. Zechariah (Graded Core Thinker, False Prophet/Satan): White Christmas, Herald
God Made, Abraham by High Marriage Commuting Interval
Galatians, Marriage Love, 1 to Many, God Ministry (Dollar the Brain, High Tither)(2xWhite Dragon False Security Banking 白龙王,王八/Phoenix Fasci UN Luohan 凤凰/乌鸦) in Utopia, the Blessing of God. Hell (Upside Down Heaven, Caesar Polar Banknote, Labour) Route
Extra Core 5 (Universal Standard e.g. not 5C but 5V) in 24 Heaven (Free Rental Security Premium, Currency Packets, toward Oriental Promised Land)
Fasci UN, Chinese Security Bank Vulnerable in TW/MY (Wireless Weapon) *64
Tiananmen, Campaign against University Flooding (Tsunami Conspiracy) 楚汉争霸武林至尊兵马俑

Inaugural Ancestry 种族 (Dust Made 尘作)
Jewish 新华: Jude Diaspora (Prophet) vs Jew Indigenous (False Prophet)
Virginia the Scapegoat: Due to Critics of Royalty the Betrayer
Levi 珠江: Scapegoat, Prime Indigenous

iii. Ezra (Extra Core Doer, False Christ/Serpent): Holy Night, Christmas Nativity
King Made, Abraham by Marriage & Carrier, Realism Marriage Tither High Interval
Corinthians, True Love, the Many to Many, Christian Ministry (Pound the Brick, Time Metric by Meta Merge), (Flying Dragon Freelance 小龙,金刚/Dark Dragon Underground 乌龙,暴龙) in Heaven, the Won't Failed Miracle.
Renaissance (Dead End Mileage, Business) Route
Graded Core 3 (Marriage Tither Long Break) in 24 Heaven (Low Duty Agency by Multiply Flagship to Treasure Blueprint, WYSIWYG with Patience)
ISIS Nazi, Global Class Agency Headquarter, Villain Meta in SG/CN (Remote Conference)

WWII, Conspiracy of Control Shanghai the Anti Villain Meta. "Orthogonal Religion 'Small Naughty Child' Atomic Bomb against Japan Buddhism Cult", 黄巾之乱桃园结义三请茅庐
Final Clan 籍贯 (Quantum Made 云作)
Hebrew 满族: High Biblical Meta Capita (Labour) vs Low Biblical Meta Capita (Business)
Virginia the Gentile: Due to Wall Revival for Loyalty as low as Misconduction of Business
Welsh 福建: Gentile, Prime Outsider

*Landing Timeline of Unlocked these 21per Solar Heaven "Lock6, The 1 Decade Age Locked", Before 1 year, 100days interval, the Great Normalised Orbit, G.N.O.

I. Cold War, Security Instrument (Wooded 木材) vs Heritage Instrument (Timbered 伐木), Ukraine & Russian Tension on Economy of Carrier Congression Dispute i.e. Anti Semitc

Ether Prophet (ESD 6G, Horse the Unicorn Offspring, Non Real Meta the High Commuting) &
Malachi (EMF 4.5G, 50per Lambda Puppet, Real Meta Non Commuting Colony) False Prophet
Transformer 造云人 Quantum Sky/Unicorn 独角兽 ESD Nerve High Gain Energy Rewards

Carrier (Cold War Parachute): E.T. 未来人 (Fox) & Apollo 太空人 (Messi the Flagship of Fox Footprint) vs Chang'er 嫦娥 (Puppy) & Spiderman 蜘蛛侠 (Sky High, Moon)

Pneumatic Control Car vs Electric Control Car
IBM Modular Universal Machine vs Apple Scalar Metallurgy Component
Security Instrument (Wooded 木材) vs Heritage Instrument (Timbered 伐木)

Remote Place, Low Capita, Gross Capital Federation, Geneva Academy
Metropolis
Olive Tree Road, Canyon Road, Silk Road
Fasci Mafia, Tsunami Prime UN, Private/Spy Remote Place

II. Civil War, Nehemiah (Israel Wall, Islam vs Lutheran Politic Dispute) False
Prophet Suit vs Zecharish (All Cold War, Jew, Jude, Levi Family Dispute)
False Prophet Suit (Christian Treasure Blueprint Prime Closure of Carrier)

Nehemiah (UV 5.5G, Seismic, Lion the True Love Hunter) Prophet &
Zechariah (UV 3.5G, 99per Epsilon Sheppard Dog, False Prophet (Scapegoat
the Whitelist Stellar Head)

Quantum Sky (Civil War Dog Fight): Queens (Rabbit) & Jesuit the Seal
matched to Queen Issued/Kings (Batman 蝙蝠侠) & Royal Professional (Cat
龙猫)
(18per Chinese Luohan Monks i.e. UN Chancellor, 99per Lost & Found
Sheep vs 1per Islam Stellar Head (False Prophet)
(Deep Sea, Mars)

Ancient Dragon Couples 19th Pair vs Theology Flagship (Milk Feeds vs Bear
Fruits)
High Ranking Estate, Land Property Value vs High Federal per Capita i.e.
GDP due Islam Deficit Grant Free Islam Royal Hierarchy the Global
Financial Deficit Special Grants

Laboratory Agency, Medium Capita, Gross Capital Federal, High Economic
Wall
Fig Tree Road Merge Beach Road i.e. Mile End Road, Global Class Fountain
(Nazi Whitelist, Genocide Prime ZION, President/Chief Headquarter)

III. World War, Harbour Dust (World War Ant Wall), Christian Natalie
(Christian Duty per Capita) vs Fundamentalist Intellect (Gross Tither Duty)
a.k.a. Quantum Weapon one of 16 kinds of Dust Ultra Sonic Ray. i.e. RF

Ezra (ESD 3G, Ancient Dragon the 101th Lamb the Newborn Anointed or
Non Newborn Incarnated) False Prophet
Habakkuk (EMF 5G, Sigma Pekinese) Prophet

Harbour Dust (World War Ant Wall): Trojan Host (Owl the Snowman U.F.O.
Biblical Ultra Low Capita the Refugee & Apollo) vs Net Bus (666 Sigma
Scapegoat, Whitelist 6 Meta Merger High Lambda Capita Dragon (Chris,
Signature Traits of Monalisa), Blacklist)
(Outer Space, Planet #3)

Carrier or Marriage Duty Ransom Lawsuit vs Mafia the Love or Carrier
Criminal
Rehab, Prison, High Biblical Capita Town, Schism Road i.e. Rehab
Federal Suburbs, International Marketplace, Fashioned Hall, Airport Road
i.e. Prison
(Qing Organised, Hijacked Prime Security Fund, Chancellor/Pope Palace)

Devil works with The Remark: (Founder of False Doctrine that Colonisation of Donkey the Gentile in Outer Space i.e. Alternate Core->**Natural Death**->Earth in Heaven (Fire Lake)
The Stellar Head to Montage of Islam, the Remark Dragon.

False Christ works with The Baptist: (Harvest Erotic from False Royalism) – Terrorism & Repentance People->Word Prison->**Vegetable Death**->Genocide->Parallel World (Fire Lake)
2nd Clause or Closure: False Anabaptism most the time the Pilgrim of Idol the Dalai Lama typically, in which the Holy Spirit was Cast Out (The Degraded or Derivative) from Tither the Extra Core, rather than Self Tailoring the Graded Core by Self Judification of Class Grading.

Satan works with The E.T. : (Harvest Power of Economic Conspiracy) – Tsunami because of False Ministry cause Economic Loss->Trojan Horse->Erotic Defect into Revenge->**Sudden Death** (Mental Treatment)->Hell Prison->Reincarnation (2nd Resurrection)

Serpent works with The Demon & Eve: (Cornerstone of Blind Faith that Postpone Civilisation Maturity)->**Sudden Death** (2nd Resurrection)

Man of Sins works with The Joker: Vegetable Death (Harvest Money from Word Ransom)->Oppose Economy Progress->Vegetable Death->(1st Resurrection)

False Prophet works with The King: (Legacy of Colonisation of Donkey)->Genocide->Colony->Sabotage into Prison->**Suicide** (Terror)->Vanished->Hell (Fire Lake)

Errata 23Jan2023

Y278. The Ending of Biblical Villain II: The Penalty of Secular World (Broadcast)

Devil works with The Remark: (Founder of False Doctrine that Colonisation of Donkey the Gentile in Outer Space i.e. Alternate Core->**Natural Death**->Earth in Heaven (Fire Lake)
The Stellar Head to Montage of Islam, the Remark Dragon.

False Christ works with The Baptist: (Harvest Erotic from False Royalism) – Terrorism & Repentance People->Word Prison->**Vegetable Death**->Genocide->Parallel World (Fire Lake)
2nd Clause or Closure: False Anabaptism most the time the Pilgrim of Idol the Dalai Lama typically, in which the Holy Spirit was Cast Out (The Degraded or Derivative) from Tither the Extra Core, rather than Self Tailoring the Graded Core by Self Judification of Class Grading.

Satan works with The E.T. : (Harvest Power of Economic Conspiracy) – Tsunami because of False Ministry cause Economic Loss->Trojan Horse->Erotic Defect into Revenge->**Sudden Death** (Mental Treatment)->Hell Prison->Reincarnation (2nd Resurrection)

Serpent works with The Demon & Eve: (Cornerstone of Blind Faith that Postpone Civilisation Maturity)->**Sudden Death** (2nd Resurrection)

Man of Sins works with The Joker: Vegetable Death (Harvest Money from Word Ransom)->Oppose Economy Progress->Vegetable Death->(1st Resurrection)

False Prophet works with The King: (Legacy of Colonisation of Donkey)->Genocide->Colony->Sabotage into Prison->**Suicide** (Terror)->Vanished->Hell (Fire Lake)

Errata 23Jan2023

Volume 2: The Fringes of Final Inter-World Competes.

Clergy or Technie

Jesuit Economy Treasure Focus: From Promised Land to Adventist

Classification of Ethnic: Ethnic Labelling & Graded
Politics Evolution: Series to Economic Harvest Reinvention
Christian Politics: Social Science
Christian Medicine: Genealogy Technology

Y470. Classification Of Ethnic VII: The Ethnic Nativity Milestone, Correspond the Official Time Zone (Census)

A. **Jacob Generations** (Final): 4x Dragon & 24x Leaders, 1x Antichrist (Metallic, Green)
123456 - Program Literacy – Goal Solving – Protocol Language
Low Level English, High Level Chinese – Japanese
Lambda λ, Theta θ (Star Dust Collector) – Genetic Correlation – Eye (Pilot)(Auto Pilot)
Canaan (Jew) – Jacob
Judah vs Chinese – **Lilith Eve's Lord (Holy See)** (Marxism Socialist)
New Canaan a.k.a. Israel i.e. **Hebrew** (Celt) - **Jacob II** (Monarchy), Israel
Offspring: Joshua/James
Chinese Medicine: Vectorial Genetic (Nativity Correlation), Chemical Topical Drug, Sterilised – Carbon Reaction (Holistic)
Acute Organ Failure, Tumour Cells & Cancer Cells i.e. UV Disease (Standard Exposure)

B. **Abraham Generations** (Induced): Goat, 3x Scapegoat (Gland, Pink)
ABC - Operation Literacy – Golden Rules – Body Language
Low Level English, Low Level Chinese – English
Sigma Σ, Psi ψ (Cryptography Load) – Genetic Inheritance – Heart (Manual)
Israelite vs Asian – **Abraham** (Nationalist) – **Abraham Wife Sarah, Egyptian**, (Fascism Socialist)
Jewish vs Roman – The Elder Son of Abraham, **Jacob** Offspring: Jesuit
Levi vs Germanic– The Brother of Jacob, Offspring: Chris
Therapy Medicine: mDNA Cryptography a.k.a. Stemcell (Chronography Correlation), Resonance & Radiation, Pasteurised – Toxic Residue (Pentecostal)
Cancer Organ i.e. ESD Disease (High Voltage Footage)

C. **Noel Generations** (Original): Lamb i.e. Ace, Gentile (Creamy, Yellow)
Banana - Assembly Literacy – Data Benchmark – Crypto Language
High Level English, Low Level Chinese – Chinese
Gamma Γ, Pi π (Quantum Carrier) – Holy Spirit Incarnation – Brain (Pilot)
Canaan (Jew) – Joseph (Oriental Democracy)
Egyptian vs Islamic – Joseph's Family (Democrat Socialist)
Judah (Jude) Canaan (Jew)– Last Man, Joseph Offspring (Republican): Messi
Pharmacy Medicine: DNA Chromosome (Footage Correlation), Specific Chemistry Structure Tempered – Hormone Radiation (Homogenous)
Mind Poison to Chronic Nerve Disorder i.e. EMF Disease (Existence Undenied)

D. **Adam Generations** (Coherent): Sheep, 1x Lost Sheep (Ceramic, Blue)
Do Re Mi - Parametric Literacy – Law Constitution – Emotion Language

High Level English, High Level Chinese – Korean

Alpha α, Beta β (Imperial Footage) – Holy Spirit Conceived – Ear (Auto)
Clay by Image of God,

1st Man vs Jude – **Adam** (Goat, Sky Pentecost) (Democracy), Omega Ω: Santa Claus

Rib of Man – 1st Women, **Eve (Lamb, Moon)**, also the Last Women. Breath - Holy Spirit

Semitic (**Egyptian**): Eve Offspring

Surgery Medicine: RNA Gene (Timer Correlation), Specific Enzyme to Generic Enzyme

Annealing – Nicotine Static Wave (Orthogonal)

Heart Inflammation to Lung Infection i.e. IR Disease (Technology Maturity)

Errata 2Feb2023, Errata 25Dec2022

Y534. Classification Of Ethnic VIII: Heaven Elections as well as Theology Treasure Pillar & Foundation (Census)

The Three Carrier per Continent and 3 Viral Villain Schism the Correlation

A. 黄, Lamb 圣哉, 猎人 vs Gentile 四活物, 月宫 (满清政权, 满洲黑龙 Anointed vs 炎黄, 宫廷 Lock Dragon) 治水, 珠江, 珍珠: Israelite the Jacob Rolls, Nile River 尼罗河 – Royalism->Medicine WHO/NASA/WWF (Projection Blueprint the Metrology)
Polish the Catholic: 满 满洲 (救赎论 Redemption), 朝鲜人 Chosen (Pelangan the Loyalty Free Academy Education Free with Non Church Tither)
Dutch the Episcopal: 庆 重庆 (象征论 Tither), 匈奴人 Korean (*Datok* the Duty Free with Inheritance of Legacy) & Non Church Tither)
French the Fundamentalist: 荆 黑龙江(神学论 Atonement), 东洋人 Japanese (Batik the License Free & Free Lawsuit with Non Church Tither)
Germanic the Gross Schism: 客 湘州 (怀疑论 Schism), 汉族人 Kanji (Rabbi with Church Tither)
Germans the Vatican: 闽 厦门 (爱情进化论 Diplomacy e.g. Marriage Tither in Ring number), 蒙古人 Mongolia (Office Army & University Scholar Free with Non Church Tither)

B. 琼, Sheep 独角兽, 牧羊人 vs Antichrist 以利亚先知, 阴间 (汉室, 朝廷 Couple or Model vs 楚国, 诸侯 Scholar or Nazi Business) 蝗灾, 黄河, 海鲜: Hebrew the Abraham Series, Galilea Sea 加利利海 – Democrat->Security CIA/FBI/ZION (Graded Blueprint the Criminology)
Anglo the Regime Repel, Deep Sea 琼 White Sea Coral Sea 日本海
Irish, Coral Island 温 Yellow Sea Deep 南中国海
Gothic, Isles 杭 Red Sea Strait 东海
Welsh, Yellow River 浙 Deep Sea 黄河
Scottish the Cells Schism, River 苏 Gland Sea 长江
British the Royal Traitor, Strait 京 White River 古黑龙江

C. 桂, Goat 牧羊犬, 羊群 vs Scapegoat 六头兽, 十二果实树 (太阳的后裔, 明太子 Biblical Identical vs 华夏, 疆域 Gentile) 野火, 长江, 盐湖: Jewish the Adam Generations, Jordan River 约旦河 – Democracy->Theology UN/KMT/NATO (Cast Out Blueprint the Heritage)
Canaan i.e. Arabian 壮
Levi i.e. Aboriginal 粤
Jude i.e. Diaspora 津
Latin i.e. Egyptian 疆
Greek i.e. Indigenous 府
Roman i.e. Persian 潮

Theology Foundation:
Graded Core: Tither Flagship e.g. COSMOS, Universe Cryptography
Alternate Core: Islam Ally Flagship e.g. NASA, Clinical Modular Layering
Extra Core: Buddhism Ally Flagship e.g. CNSA, Universal Constant

Errata 8Feb2023

Y516. Political Evolution IX: Bi-partisan Congress, 3 People Principle, Tither Tax of Servant (Census)

A. Fix the African Democracy **Mistake the 1st**.
911 Lessons
Terrorism of Bottomline Natalie, due Contemporary Culture influence Social Disorder.
Politic correlation: **Bi-partisan Congress**, Democrat Socialist to Join Chinese. Resolution to Mafia Guinea.
Execution Plan: **Auditing the Islam Funding in World Bank.**
Biblical Villain Fitting Test: Devil, the Space Agency of Japan, the Bi-partisan Congress Chairman to Reserve the African Equality, all phase by Semitic Persecution.

B. Fix the Chinese Royalism Democrat. **Mistake the 2nd**.
64 Generations
Colony of Natalie due University Academy Hierarchy.
Politic correlation: 50 States totalitarianism into **3 People Principle**.
Constitutional Resolution to Climate Change.
Execution Plan: **Auditing the Scammed Chinese Congress Chancellor.**
Biblical Villain Fitting Test: 4th Person the King Caesar. Marxism Nazi, Genocide against Christian Chinese, i.e. Christian Persecution. The Islam Judgement Taliban. Man of Sins i.e. Royal Doctor, Korea Traitor.

C. Fix the Nationalist Constitutional **Mistake the 3rd**.
311 Series
Mafia the No Devotion Christian Chinese.
Politic correlation: **Tither Tax of Servant** into Holistic Medicine. Calendar Axis Break-in to Pandemic Resolution.
Execution Plan: **Auditing the Weapon & Cutting Edge Military focused Treatment Investment.**
Biblical Villain Fitting Test: Contemporary Business Misconduction against Populated, e.g. Telecommunication Scamming, to name the Primary. i.e. False Christ, the Man Made.

D. Maintain the Republican Socialist Elections Precaution the Primary. **And No More.**
Covid-19 Programs
Germans Election the Ecumenical ruler from Villain.
Politic correlation: Resolution to Full Gospel Redemption. Leave as it.
Execution Plan: **Auditing the Salvation of Guinea, Germans Calendar Progression of Advent.**
Biblical Villain Fitting Test: False Prophet the Lambda Carrier, against the Western Civilisation Leading, throw in Testing.
Copyright (C) 2023, Ryan Lai Hin Wai, All right reserved.

Y518. Politic Evolution X: The Chancellor & Congress Elections (Census)

Ruler Grading
The Congress

Pyramid
the Capacity
and Capita Rating
Datum starred, Democrat Capita
Margin remark, Democracy Capita
Profit highlight, Royal Capita

Hybrid Pyramid
So on.

The Reaction
4 Medicine & 4 Energy

Combustion Reaction
Chemistry electrolysis Reaction
Fusion Reaction
Organism Reaction
Globalisation Axis
The Capita Regime
Capita Carrier
Capita Pyramid
Social Structure and Carrier Structure
Hybrid Pyramid Pilot
Nationalist Mafia East to West
The Nazi and Anti Nazi, blended.
English Native or Chinese Native.
Pilot

In illustration,

4 Congress Symbol

A. The 'R' footprint – Mileage ->Tax Law -> Economic Congress
B. The '+' crossed – Duty -> Labour Law -> Judi Congress
C. The '*' starred – Montage -> Constitutional Law -> Climate Congress
D. The ',' dotted – Pilot -> Business Misconduction Law -> Semitic Congress

Y258. Christian Politic I: Military, Academic, Religion (Census)

A. Matthew Gospel | Apostle Presbyterian/Eastern Orthodox/Lutheran | Transformer Jesus

+

A. John Gospel | Angel/Witch vs Catholic Church | St Joseph/Mary/Joshua |
Daily Bread Book->Ward |

WHO, Business School (Italian)(Dessert)(Mafia):
Fudan; National Taiwan; Singapore National; Melbourne; London School of Economics; Harvard
(Reinventing Blueprint vs Reverse Engineering Replica), John the Baptist (Virus Proof)

B. Mark Gospel | Alien/Jinn vs Episcopal Church |
Seagull/Messiah/James |
Stream in the Desert Book->Mental |
WWF, University (France)(Range)(Organised Syndicate):
Shanghai Jiao Tong; National Chiao Tung; Nanyang; Adelaide; Cambridge; Stanford
(Ultimate Theory Prediction vs Pseudo Science Projection), Elijah (Nuclear Proof)

C. Luke Gospel | Predator/Owl vs Charismatic Church |
Jehovah/Christ/Santa Claus |
365 days Bible->Prison |
NASA, Institute (Germany)(Tropical)(Cult Syndicate):
Tsinghua; National Chengchi; Ngee Ann; Brisbane; Oxford; Massachusett
(Experimental Strategy Diplomacy vs Simulation Analysis Solution),
Solomon (Tsunami Proof)

Errata 14Aug2022

Y441. Christian Politics XIII: 6 Time Division Chronicle Seismic Station (Census)

A. The Axis, 5000 Years (normalised Pre A.D. 5000): Israel Civilisation, Jewish to Jew Community Hierarchy Spread over the Western Continent and Island.
Seismic Station: Japan Imperial Palace (Jerusalem), UN
Pre A.D. 5000 to A.D. 1 (i.e. Post 5000 Years)
(**Canyon Road**, Devil, **Terrorism** Think Tank Catholic, *A.D. 1943*), Meta 3 (Post Pentecost, Apostolic)

B. 1 billion Years (normalised Old A.D. 10000): India Civilisation, Himalayan to Mediterranean Ethnic Hierarchy Spread over the Asia Continent and Island.
Seismic Station: Russia Pentagon Hawaii (Shangri la), NATO
Old A.D. 10000 to A.D. 1 (i.e. Throwback 1 billion Years)
(**Babel Tower**, False Christ, Fund Economic Crisis for **Tsunami**, *A.D. 1943*), Meta 4 (Quantum, Pentecostal)

C. 2000 Years (normalised A.D. 500): Roman Civilisation, Jewish to Jew Community Hierarchy Spread over the Europe Continent and Island.
Seismic Station: Singapore Istana Palace (Persia), WWF
A.D. 500 to A.D. 1500 (i.e. Post 2000 Years)
(**Berlin Wall**, Satan, **Colony** Sabotage, *A.D. 1694*), Meta 3 (Post Pentecost, Apostolic)

D. 0.5 billion Years (normalised B.C. 5000): Egyptian Civilisation, Germans to Anglo Community Hierarchy Spread over the Western Continent and Island.
Seismic Station: Korea Blue House (Catholic), KMT
B.C. 5000 to B.C. 1 (i.e. Throwback 0.5 billion Years)
(**Great Wall of China**, Serpent, **Cult** Regime Scapegoat, B.C. 3057), Meta 2 (Pentecost, Vatican)

E. 0.25 billion Years (normalised New A.D. 250): Mayan Civilisation, Germans to Anglo Community Hierarchy Spread over the America Continent and Island.
Seismic Station: United States White House (Vatican), NASA
A.D. 1750 to A.D. 2000 (i.e. Post 0.25 billion Years)
(**Jerusalem Wall**, Man of Sins, Nuclear Weapon **Genocide**, *A.D. 1969*), Meta 2 (Pentecost, Vatican)

F. 10000 Years (normalised New B.C. 1000): Chinese Civilisation, Germans to Anglo Ethnic Hierarchy Spread over the Asia Continent and Island.
Seismic Station: United Kingdom Buckingham Palace (Episcopal), WHO

A.D. 1500 to A.D. 2500 (i.e. Throwback 10000 Years)
(**Silk Road**, False Prophet, **Trojan Horse** Bribery, *A.D. 2219*), Meta 1
(Biblical, Catholic)
Errata 1Dec2022

Y448. Christian Politics XX: New World Government Revolution (Census)

I. Information Distrust Act:
Olive (Milk) and Fig (Honey) Land, the Habitat Earth->7th Star, the pulling Heaven and Earth.
Trinity God, Multi-theism God Hostage:
Nativity Correlation: Utopia Alpha, Utopia Beta

II. Marriage Protection Act:
Oriental I (optional)->Oriental II
Father, Mother Candidate Hostage:
Calligraphy Carrier: Anglo, Germans, Jew

III. Human Right & Privacy Protection Act:
Promised Land->Advent
Children 14 Generations Hostage:
Chronography Pilot: Alpha, Omega, Y, Q, A, Z corresponding to Early Bird, Pioneer, Founder, Inheritor, Ancestry, Offspring

Errata 4Nov2022

A. Monarchy Candle IR vs Democrat Socialist Gland EMF
No Discrimination Public Heritage vs Redemption Private Heritage
(Poker Suit)(The Freedom Suit) vs (Mahjong Suit)(Fashion Society Suit)
Oversea Chinese Clan (Rusted Mileage, **Public R&D the Holistic Science**, Revolutionist Old Maverick)
Tionghua & Israel Repel Clan (Luxury Mileage, **NGO Regime the Diplomat Trade Boundary**, Prophet Youth Dragon Girl)

7th Heaven, Buddhism Ally (CNSA)
Transformer i.e. False Prophet
(如来佛祖, 至高圣者)(金刚, 假行僧)(小龙女, 王奶奶)(Biblical Villain, Individual Test)(e.g. The Scarecrow)
Advent, if Sigma #3, #2 Hot Pursuit
– Hell Route (Fire Lake, Kings, The Genius Scientist, Einstein, Newton)
Sigma #4 Messi 007 卫斯理 (背景: 西游记, 励志: 解密拯救)
Module Machine i.e. RC, **King Made**, Pilot, Trinity
Lambda #8 Nationalist i.e. Constitutional Lent (Jewish, CN)

Pentagon (Mafia Underground): HAWAII (ZION)(KMT)
 (World War, by take down Conspiracy Network as whole, Long runs to Rip the Sow better than delayed.)
False Royalism, War & Heritage, Empire Colonel/Royal Pope:
Racial Buddhism e.g. 净土宗禅 (五鬼八仙) vs 少林寺 (金刚罗汉)
World War/Cold War: Regime Revolution, Ecumenical Standard i.e. International Law Treaty
*1943 Pearl Harbour *911 Terrorism Hijack Politics
Heart, Diamond Holoscope, Cache, Carrier Mileage (ROM Disc, Blue Ray, Bluetooth, Radar, 4G) – Annealed (Send to B.C. 5000 Year), Israel Clan (e.g. Fruity Wine)(Against Drunk the Timer Disorder)

Imperial Palace Japan (Nazi Regime): GER (WHO)
Misconduction War & Heritage
*Preliminary Studied, Virus primary target EU (aids), HK (avian), SG (sars), CN & UK (covid)

Continue on next Page

Continued

B. Fasci Socialist Lantern EMF vs Nationalist, Chromatic IR
Atonement Public Heritage vs Black Equality Private Heritage
(Christmas Suit)(The Atonement Suit) vs (African Suit)(Noel Suit)
Israel Clan (Commuting Mileage, **Public Government the Solid Treaty**,
Hollywood Mario Fashions)
Turkey & Russia Repel, (Dead End Mileage, **Private F&B the Invoice**,
Contemporary Neck Uniforms)

7ᵗʰ Heaven, Hinduism Ally (SpaceX)
E.T., Fox/Rabbit/Owl/Cat etc. i.e. Antichrist
(昭蝉西施, 泥菩萨)(末代皇帝, 王小二)(Biblical King, Carrier Mileage Trial)(e.g.
Little Prince)
Oriental, if Sigma #2, #1 High Stake
– Mobile Route (Ghost the Scientific Body, Pairs, 4 of a Kind, Full House,
Flush, Royal Flush, the Talented Tycoon, Noel, Little Drummer Boy)
Sigma #4 Chris 007 琼瑶 (背景: 红楼梦, 励志: 加密变天)
Robot Computer i.e. AI, **God Made**, Automatic, Total Theism
Lambda #8 Nationalist i.e. Constitutional Lent (Jewish, EU)

Istana Palace (Mafia Organised): SG (NATO)(Jerusalem)
(Cold War, by Performing Ecumenical Lawsuit, Religion Authority)
Misconduction Business & Government, Jack
Levi Democracy, Tax Collector (Intellectual)(Long Terms Government)
*1976 Earth Quake Tangshan, *1986 Earth Quake SG, *2022 Footage
Frauding to Multimedia (Voided Credential Records)(Getting Collapsed for
Terrorism Upgraded, getting permission for Fasci Entering CN from MY)
Brain – Magnetic Address, Milestone (Harddisk, Wireless, Satellite, 5G) –
Tempered (Send to A.D. 1), Europe Clan, (e.g. Honey Whiskey)(Against Nerve
Chronic the Bill)

Blue House (Fasci Recruit Campaign): JPN (FBI)
False Doctrinal, Medicine & Banking, First Class Doctor):
(First Class Medicine, Non Veterinary Subjected, and Non for Profit
Medicine)
St. Paul Church (Arch Angel II) vs Charismatic
*311 Tsunami, *Year 1970-1999 Y2K Bugs Dimension, False Administration
Void System Protocol (Immune Strengthen)

Continue on next Page

Continued

C. Republican Flash ESD vs Oriental Democracy Bright UV
Intellects Marriage vs Gender Equality Marriage
(Labour Suit)(Fashion Society Suit) vs (Wendy Suit)(Babel Suit)
Europe Clan (The Luxury Mileage, **PS Regime the Free Trade Boundary**,
Prophet, Bigfoot Penthouse)
Arab & Germans Repel Clan, (Rusted Mileage, **Private R&D the Hybrid
Technology**, Revolutionist Julie Youth)

7th Heaven, Islam Ally, Utopia the Final (NASA)
Gabriel Angel, White Dragon Short i.e. False Christ
(八仙, 修道人), (Major Prophet), (Biblical Anointed)(e.g. Caesar the Welder),
Utopia, if Sigma #5, #3 The Need for Speed
- Sky Route (Pentecost the Spiritual Body, Jack the Picture, The Man Made
Inventor, Righteous Brothers, Doraemon, Edison, Tesla, Bill Gate)
Sigma #4, Jesuit 007 金庸 (背景: 三国志, 励志: 修道结义)
Scalar Machine i.e. VR, **Man Made**, Manual, Monotheism
Lambda #13 Regime i.e. Constitutional Monarchy Lent (Hebrew, US)

White House (Qing Syndicate Scapegoat *Hijack): US (UN)(NASA)
 (Civil Smoke Bomb & Internet Army Censorship vs Peace Maker, the
Telecommunication Protocol War)
False Democracy, Engineering & Education, Royal King:
Islam Capitalist Lawmakers (i.e. Mining Tycoon):
Civil War/Racial Riot: Politic Revolution, Calendar Standard i.e. Royal
Career Axis & Scale
Washington Islam Goat vs Lincoln Christian Goat
(Major/Minor/False Prophet)(Evil, Ghost, Alien, Devil, to Robot)
*1960 Apollo to Kennedy Conspiracy, 1970 Semiconductor to Elvis Presley
Conspiracy, *2000 Technology Stalled at Nuclear & Gun Treaty
Ear, Circuit Formation, Diode, Chrono (Flashdrive, Wire, Telecom, 1G) –
Sterilised (Send to B.C. 50Million Year), Asia Clan, (e.g. Smokey
Beer)(against Acute Organ Tumour the Heart Fatal Error)

Iskandar Palace (Fasci Think Tank): MY (CIA)
Misconduction Engineering & Education, Empire King
*Malay Babyboom Generation take over Hijack Politic Failed until Qing
Syndicate Take Over and Bi-partisan, ISIS-Fasci, 2018->2022.
*Crime Lawsuit against Buddhism Heritage. *1988 'Tiananmen' & 2022
'Great Wall" China Revolution against all kinds of Cult.

Continue on next Page

Continued

D. Democracy, Spot UV vs Marxism Socialist, Flash ESD
Natalie Career vs Semitic Equality Career
(Cow Bow Suit)(Arsenal Suit) vs (Business Suit)(Eden Suit)
Asia Clan (Dead End Mileage, **Public F&B the Bill**, Contemporary Pluto)
Persia & Japan Repel Clan (Commuting Mileage, **Private Government the Soft Treaty**, Disney Cartoon)

Holy See, Renaissance (The 370 Sheep to 1 Sheep) or Hiatus (The 370 Sheep to 1 Sheep)
Iron Man, White Dragon Long i.e. Devil
(土地公, 传道人)(龙王/魔王, 妖精/才女, 传道人), (Minor Prophet), (Biblical Reborn, e.g. Maria II)
Renaissance if Sigma #1, #4 Tournament
- Sea Route (Sofa, Queens, the ATM Banknote, The Legend Doctor, Lincoln, Washington, Elizabeth II)
Sigma #6 Santa Claus 007 三毛 (背景: 水浒传, 励志: 传道继承)
Flying Calculator i.e. AR, **Queen Made**, Autopilot, Partial Theism
Lambda #2 Democracy i.e. Monarchy Lent (Semitic, UK)

Buckingham Palace (Nazi Economy Body): UK (WWF)
(Racial Riot, University Intelligence Protest Against War Crime, Money Games prevent from Colony)
False Ministry, Medicine & Banking, Royal Queen:
(Public Medicine, the Veterinary)
St. Peter Church (Arch Angel I) vs Vatican
*1997 Dianna Princess Conspiracy from Military Regime. And Series of Aftermath.
Eye, Ray Burning, Footage (Fibre Optics, 3G) – Pasteurised (Send to Post A.D. 2000 Year), Tionghua Clan, (e.g. Milk Cider)(Against Cancer the Toxic informatic)

Grand Palace Thailand (Qing Syndicate Funding): THAI (World Bank)(Vatican)
Misconduction Medicine & Banking, Empire President
Germanic Regime, Loyalty Rewards, (Personnel)(Hijacked Government)
*1997 Shanghai Economic Crisis Conspiracy, and Series of Aftermath not the least linked to Nuclear triggered Climate Change, and Medicine Evolution to Veterinary. The New Weapon of Quantum lead to Faulty of Machine including Human Body, and this heading to A.I fully Autopilot.

Errata 29Dec2022

I. Adventist->Original Heaven (Fire Lake Route)

i. Philippian 青梅竹马与新不了情 Vatican Pope/Colossian Episcopal Bishop/Ephesian Catholic Rabbi Peterburg, Patriarch Stevenburg/Philemon Charismatic Evangelist

ii. Autopilot involuntary, Lock 1 Official, Generations Safari, Quartet Strings 四重奏

iii. *Women Dime i.e. Dollar* (Honours)(Credit Card)(Licenses)(Royalty, Hygienic Tax, Compensation)

iv. 古龙 vs 古惑仔 Celebrity High Meta, Timothy 红楼梦

v. Herald Eden Garden, Comet 5per Dust, e.g. Deep Sea Ecosystem Guinea Isle), 3G Archimedes (Genocide), Thermal Meta Curve Burner
- Israel Calendar (Criminal Crime)

vi. 1st Dead
Departure Ship, to Big 7th Heaven, Metrology Lock Reflective Affiliation Union

vii. *Gentile 黑天鹅 vs 龙猫 Layla Malachi, Puppet*
*Puppy Love (*War & Wall Treasure Era, Suntzi 孙子兵法) **Wall Learning*
Kiwi as Genius (George Town, Beach Town)
Gross Intellect Capital (*Won*) = (*US Origin Platform as KR 12th Arrival Gate, the Terminal)*

viii. Soul Mate Journey (1 or 4 Dating Interval->**One of a kind Church** i.e. Benchmark Coring, Router IBM Office Oracle)

ix. Fasci NATO (**Russian Underground Mafia**), ***Prophet***, ISIS Herald, the Whitelist Scapegoat, 99.5+0.5%per the Schematic Dust (0.5% Meta, Once from A to Z)
Islam Noel, Space Castle i.e. Broadcast Router, a.k.a. Security House
Buddhism End Universe, Space Castle i.e. Metrology Router, a.k.a. Investment Mall

II. Renaissance->Oriental II)(Mobile Route)

i. Titus 霸王与王八 Herald (e.g. Parish. ¼ Duty)(Puritan Music Tither, Christian Ministry)/Jude's Fundamentalist Clergy (Christian Education Tither, Christian Ministry)

ii. Manual Configuration, Lock 6 Signatured, Series Explorer, Hiphop 嘻哈

iii. *Women Token i.e. Cent* (Slots)(Cash)(Certificate)(Metro Platform)(Loyalty, Duty Fee, Salary)

iv. 黑龙/暴龙 Labour Desperado, Ezra 小刀会

v. Oriental Eden Garden, Meta 36per Cloud e.g. Hunter Peterburg Broken Arrow Wall), 4.5G Solomon (Nuclear), Ionised Magnetic Disk
- Lunar Calendar (Colony Crime)

vi. 2nd Resurrection
Mile End City, the Dragon Coach & Lion Air, Chronography Lock per Capita Biased Clan

vii. *Sheep 麻雀 vs 未来人 (not E.T) Business Philemon, Pi Unicorn the Change Environment*
*Liberal Love (Offspring Inheritor Era, 父辈遗产委托) *Meta Allergy*
Peanut as Queen (Queen Town, Isle Town)
(Hollywood, Nobels, Forbes, Oscar, Chronicle), High Natalie Capita (Pound) = (EU Origin Platform as AU 11th Arrival Gate)

viii. Multi Branch out (2 Dating Interval->**Chapel** i.e. 4 in 1, Montage Core, Crab Machine Microsoft OS, C Language)

ix. Fasci Zion, (**Nazi Organised Mafia**) ***God Father***, Blacklist Antichrist Think Tank, 99per (Best Ranked)
Islam Renaissance, Cryptography Psi Windmill i.e. Light Sky Castle, a.k.a. Uniform Camp, e.g. Sand Gallery
Buddhism Silkroad, Bandwidth Reynold Watermill i.e. Salted Lake Castle, a.k.a. Casual Cabin, e.g. Fountain Hotel

III. Utopia->Promised Land->Herald Heaven

i. Galatians 建桥与奔月 Christology Royalist (Tither Free, Public Ministry) (Supernova Route)

ii. Automatic on/off, Lock 6 Sealed, Iterative Opera, Cha-cha 恰恰

iii. *Brotherhood Sterling* i.e. Buck (Chip)(Car)(Machine)(Fare, Fellowship, Wage)

iv. 白龙 vs 忍者 Whites Chancellor, Nehemiah 梁祝

v. Original Eden Garden, 16per Coral the Supernova Cupid Stevenburg Fountain River Dust e.g. Strait the Coral Isle), 1G Newton (Terrorism), Circuit Jumper Drive
- Solar Calendar (Intelligent Duty Crime)

vi. 2nd Dead
Rocket Quantum Lock Carrier Axis, Route to Small 1st Heaven

vii. *Goat 孔雀 vs 雪人 Pi, Zechariah, Nazareth the Queen James, Fox, Understanding*
*Agape (Marriage Heritage Era, 祖宗十四代遗产委托) *Parent Preliminative*
Mint as King (Christ Town, Strait Town), High Anointed per Capita (Grand) =
(SG Origin Platform as MY 1st, Arrival Gate)

viii. Meta Documentary Story (3 Dating Interval->**Tabernacle** i.e. Hex Core, Transducer Macintosh Simulation, R Language)

ix. Qing Organised Loan Shark Mafia, 50per (always making)
Jihad **False Prophet** Islam Prayer, Wreckage Commuting i.e. Remote Village
Jihad Buddhism Non Vegetarian, Phantom Commuter i.e. Agency Estate

IV. (Heaven->Oriental I)(Black Hole Route)

i. Corinthian 牛津与图强 Pentecostal Chancellor (Tither Olive Account, God Ministry)/Thessalonian's Anglican Pastor/Ether

ii. Pilot voluntary, Lock 9 Flagship, Rollup Firefox, Sentimental 麻醉

iii. *Brotherhood Pound* (Jewellery)(Condominium)(Enclosure)(Lent, Burden, Bond)

iv. 卧龙 vs 乌龙 Preacher, Hebrew 英雄

v. Locked Eden Garden, 14per Organic the Sky e.g. Pearl Harbour River the Virgin Isle, the Aged Lock or Meta Lock), 5G Einstein (Tsunami), Blueray Histogram Burner
- Weather Calendar (Meta Crime)

vi. 1st Resurrection
Oriental Express Train Demography Lock Family Schematic Credential, to Chinese 4th Heaven

vii. *Lamb 凤凰/ 霹雳鸟 Gator, Habakkuk, Chang'er*
*Holiness True Love (Ancestry Legacy Era 祖先遗产委托) *Theology Exchange Pineapple as Servant (Holland Town, China Town), High Generic per Capita (Pound) = (TW Origin Platform as HK 8th Arrival Gate, the Inaugural)*

viii. Rolling Pursuit Battle (5 Dating Interval->**Cathedral** i.e. Quad Core, Good Patience, Olive Rolls, Jumper Bios, Assembly Language)

ix. Fasci UN, ***Dalai Lama*** 18 Rohs, 101th (Alpha & Omega Olive Dust)
Islam Eden Garden Account i.e. Rabbi, Pre-Baptism i.e. Public Clinic a.k.a. Passover
Buddhism Tither Account i.e. Parish, Post-Baptism i.e. Private Laboratory a.k.a. Tabernacle

Errata 22Feb2023

Y443. Christian Politics XIV: 6 Politic Credential Mark (Census)

A. Broadcast Weapon Licence or Intelligence Software Licence
Portrayed Timepiece vs Finger Ring – Marriage & Divorce Consensus

B. Military Academy or University College
Portrayed Cap vs Gown – Graduate Testimony

C. Bottom Community vs Diaspora Refugee
Portrayed Bell vs Tree – Certificate Addressed

D. Cult vs Formal Church
Portrayed Tie vs Ribbon – Church Fellowship

E. Mafia Trained vs Inhouse Developed
Portrayed Ear Ring vs Foot Ring – Anticipated Career Prize Award

F. Investment inclined Terrorism or Non Legacy inclined Holdings
Portrayed Towel vs Belt – Government Business Rewards

Errata 28Nov2022

Y571. The Commuting of Love 爱的进行式 (Forum)

Song of Hymns

爱的进行式 The Commuting of Love

Marriage Duty is Cowboy duty
Servant
Consular?
Teacher maybe
Carrier Loading is wholly.
Same exactly to Carrier Duty
Marriage is War and Wall of breakdown or revival depend on clever.
Not about War in Family, not Wall in Family.

About War in other Country, and Wall in stranger.
Security Value the Meta Tither Value

Copyright (C) 2023, Ryan Lai Hin Wai, All right reserved.

Y460. Christian Medicine VIII: Corner Stone of Rocket Science projection to Genealogy Medicine (Journal)

Forgiveness doesnt mean acceptance. Yellow Ribbon mean Forgiveness giving to Whole Party. The Godfather is Democracy Religion. The Hymn is Monarchy Religion Politic.

The Islam lack conditions of Warrant to be Corner stone. Its the New Party make the Warrant for Islam.

Same thing goes to Christianity. Atonement of Cross is one kind of Warrant. It is Spiritual, Natal and Credit, and Formula.

In which the Formula is sensitive and misleading tendency. This is the Crew i.e. the Sailor is Corner stone.

Degraded Formula terminated at Renaissance only, forbidden from Atonement of Cross.
Formula cannot be Corner stone.

Jesus, Israel and Moon Flag is the only Corner stone, origin, path and destination.
Islam is the loading as well as free load to Heaven. Not Corner stone.

India is not the Path, but the Alternative Route to heaven. Not Corner stone either.
Religion Unity is the Path only.

UK oppose Religion Unity. This makes them rule out from the Games of Jew and Jude.
The Last Resort is the degraded plan. Path is the Priority.

Let talk about Wealth Building. Its about Public and Private. Public Wealth is Common Wealth. Private Wealth are those transferable Wealth.

As we know, most prestige wealth until present day are non transferable. Who intentively censored this property are bearing alot of duty.

And this duty is absolute positive. Hence the Wealth will only growing. Another sense called Atonement of Jesus.

The Enemy are those Make Inverted Cross more inverted. This is the Time Theory of Wealth in-regardless Paper or Stone.

Toxic is like the Mercury, but Wealth is like the Salt. All toxic are same but all drug are against each other. And this is the Original to Final Wealth.

Same as you think.

Well, it has to be like that, this is the breakthrough. The Schism of Holy Spirit since A.D. until today. Debating the Same issue.

The Matthew Gospel, Mark, Luke, and John Gospel debate. In turns this is about Climate Law, Humanity Law, Weapon Law, and Hygienic Law.

In turns this can also projection into Nationalism, Capitalism, Commonwealth and Communism Economy.

The fundamental no changed. The Pentateuch, in which the Fifth Law is Religion Unity Law.

The Apostle Acts. Corresponding to the Nehemiah Law. In which you agree with Islam Ally. Or Buddhism Ally, is Ezra Law.

The Two Key person in Apostle Acts is Peter and Paul. St Paul and St Peter. Jump conclusion this is the way we brew the 7th Solar.

Hence, the Islam Ally is not Beta, its the only way. Of course, it is duality shifting with Buddhism ally, in sync.

This is the theory of Combustion. Comet, Supernova, and Earth. The small loop is the biggest loop.

And we could be the centre of Universe. Supernova and Comet are around us, in Hidden forms.

And this is how the star dust time disruption. Automatic.

Once we formed up the Social Structure and Heritage Law. The Food & Energy part is automatic.

This is the Promised Land, we can claim.

It is competing, unfortunately. There 45 slot, only 39.5 is max. This is relatively, of course.

The Duality God concept yields. Advent vs Oriental I,II. In fact, all are cored in piece.
The piece of Land.

1G to 7.2G. Noted that 7.2 meant 21G. Its arbitrary. No meaning. But a reference.
Less is precise.

Bad thing is accurate. Then the Peace conspiracy theory arise. The United Nations forms after WWII.

Hence Anti Semitic, Anti God so on yield. Peace, you need to pay the Price. For God Protection is free.

But condition is Caesar Tax. You pay Rent you protected. Same thing applied to our Health Care.

High Maintenance is required. The Body Timer, is triggered if you modified it. But it is nevertheless can get optimal stage.

Same thing to the Environment, it is high Lent. Those Obey Nehemiah Law get excepted from Detained.

Those can enjoy free clock. Free tax Land. This is the methodology to account the Population.

Those toxics grouped. And drug is the quantum. Meaning, All Chronicle are centralised too.

The Head counts represented the Heritage. One in Three and Three in One. Those hidden heritage are Eden Garden.

Black Hole Era remembered? All Chronicle in one whole piece land. Jurassic?

So the Mission is clear. To salvation those in Black Hole. 2G maybe. When you get 7G dont proud, people might get 21G.

Gravity is just Quantum Number. Don't use the Sharp eye. 2R, 4R or 6R footage?
There is stalled of Colour.

End Mile Road.

When you carrier is false, you never reached. Its not burner. To make quantum 7 or quantum 8 is more realistic.

7.0 to 7.1G. Practical to Theory. No Experimental. Quantum 7.1. is Biblical. All Fictional Story are no China.

There is Jew God or Jude God from Chronicle to End. Abraham and Moses God.
Israel God is Climate God.

Islam worship Abraham, and this person make American success. No thief theory. So it is a blind law to follow for justice.

And justice is just this. Whatever it shouldn't be Active Justice. It had to dive deep to repair. And this is the Quantum Number Game.

From Maze runner against the Nature Disaster, and to Circus Game. This is the Experimental Cant tell.

People now use Hall Mark, Kelvin Mark and Data Mark. There is bullshit, if no result.
For Data Mark is 100% concise.

But due to the Colour Blind, we had to compromised. The Four Era of Chronicle are Supernova, Comet, Earth and Black Hole.

And priority is on the Black Hole. The reason is 1/36G happened. The First Noel.
And bad thing cannot more than 3 times. 2G is safe. This is theory of Digital.

Is Red or White. This makes the Pink. Digital correlation is Quantum. So this can make 2R Footage. No more true Colour.

Its Set of Law, not Morality Law. The Graded Moses Law is Quantum Number. And Quantum 10 is Max.

For Climate Protocol. Seismic Graded. It is Islam Law. 9 is bad. Too bad. Convert the Quantum Number into Empirical Formula is the Iteration Step.

We called it 2 fold, 3 fold, so on. More than five is ridiculous. Yes Ancient people scare the Dark Age.

I tell you, it is about Piece of Land. The Digital Correlation make Space Overlapping.
So all this is the fundamental of Population Census.

Heritage is forever growth no limit. But those privatised are grouped in one hand.
The Free Duty Heritage.

Those Transferable Property is Revenge Mission. This Yield the Monarchy Politic until today.

This kind of property merging and growing. The Pyramid. But the Milk and Honey Land can raise Many People. This is no Pyramid but Planetary System.

It is undertaking. And lose it fast is best strategy. The Stair Case to Heaven. It is one man show. Hence yield the Rainbow 6.

Quantum 12 is a poker. It depends on the Star Dust, entire. Ether. Brief, the Universe is 2D correlation only. Newton 1st Law always right.

When there is Universe, there is thief. And this thief is only temporary. The greater one is the Black Hole.

Against the Black Hole is all of us. It is a pull river game. Black Hole is also Supernova.
Sapphire type and Jade type.

When Sapphire loses contact with Earth, it power fade. IR must not waste. And the Cold Jade Supernova, is Candle Light.

Green UV is Superpower. It is could be turn into Blackhole. The duty is to growth land, by Road Protocol. Mexico Wall for example.

Don't do stupid thing. It had to be Black and White. From there the Mining industry boom up.

This is the Whole Truth of Kelvin Mark. The Supernova Planet Approach. And this phenomenon is once in a life time.

The Processor Temperature become Cold Down. It always 45-65celcius. But Absolute Kelvin Mark lower down.

This saves the Global Warming, due to Pandemic. So, when Kelvin Mark lower down, the Pandemic Relived.

At maximum squeeze allowable. Hence the Geothermal dispersed, we could have better health.

So the UV get reduced. When ask what is Kelvin Mark? This is Happiness Index. It determines mining and crude oil. old become new, new become old.

One time only. It is a Real Number, the Pi. So when three time right, it is booming.
So one time right sufficient.

Bad thing required 3 times. Good thing just required 1 time. Its hard to get quantum 24.
but easy to get quantum 30. the 13 month.

Called White Christmas. It is automatically. The Promised Land formed.

Step is get quantum 30. Moses Law iteration 30 times. It is a new platform. The 13 month Tax make us rich.

It is pull apart from third world and first world. The Rescue of Third World and First World.

Third World became First World. First World become Utopia. The Comet Alpha, Beta, and Final. And the Third World are those Comet Beta.

From the Speed we can determine. This required Biblical comment. Every Comet is unique.

Matthew 26:55-56. Hence, it has thousand and more thousand.

This is the Camera bluff you. We need an Orthography Navigation thence can determine the Comet.

Turn the James Webb 180deg. Something applied to those Liberal Country. No Metropolis City are those Liberal Country.

Meaning this country is the Parallel Remote, e.g. Bermuda Triangle. and It's the Coral Island, fixed location never moved.

This differentiates the Comet and Asteroid. We have to address every asteroid, and plot out the Horoscope.

This tells the Kelvin Mark, the Magnetic Maturity. Meaning the Coral Island Formation, tell the Moses Number, the Current Climate.

Moses 30 is perfect. It can accommodate 125Billion Population. 5000^3. Population and Heritage arent equal.

Population is Food & Energy. Heritage is Oppose of this. So when there are more population, the more hidden heritage the free duty.

Caution, population control is not food control. Nor energy price war. Its not to build more Infrastructure either.

Its about scattering of Heritage e.g. Bible into scattering House. The ideal methodology is God made Salvation by Protection of Heritage.

This is just like Heritage Booming. To achieve that we need to identify the High Booming Heritage.

Let all growth good and bad. There Harvest can make. Why are you Dilemma? With Little Blind, we will fly.

Devotion Faith vs Blind Faith. This is Altitude and Aptitude. No Blind Faith in doing Ministry for God.

But don't worry, all this is Automatic. Unless you reject. The Imperial rule this. When I say this is for rescue.

No end loop, by the way. There is only one and only end lop in chronicle. All have to go.
Until the Forever.

This applied to any Individual. One crisis in life only. Once victory is forever victory. This is Medicine Renaissance.

The reason behind is due to Ergonomic Standard. Comet or Asteroid. And Asteroid formation, could make a new Galaxy.

This is just liked the Identity of Earth Map. 30 Horoscope in total. Heritage is forever. Called Eternal life. But this life is distanced from gentile.

When this also meant the Life span. There is end loop for each life. Make a little jump, the Normal Life to Spiritual Life, and Spiritual Life to Eternal Life, Spirit Maturity is their Meta Form.

The is only one kind of Psi. and one kind of Spirit. Spirit Generation is Spirit Maturity.
From the Fig tree to Olive.

We have to learn the spirit generation, this is about Copyright. To divide good and bad is from the Toxic or Drug.

Drug is original, coherent and final. Toxic against all this. But don't worry toxic has only little small edge in Chronicle Heritage. This is the New Finding.

All good and bad have to be harmony. You cannot differentiate it until it Boom. There are thousand and thousand of Unique Drug.

Pearl colour and Ruby Colour. 2 type. Ruby colour for treatment. Pearl colour for pro-long.

Pearl drug is unique. The Ruby drug is generic. And generic drug has harm, if no exercise.

All generic drug do treatment. all kind. The standard defines by Active or Passive Mechanism.

All Enzyme are generic but deviate by Vibration Mode. The Chemistry Cryptography Structure. This is about the Filtered.

The typical Vibration mode is 6.8 protocol. 50+4 Network. This is Heritage and Climate, and Weapon.

Of course, its Annealed by Sigma. This is each individual spiritual embodiment.
When the branch injured, all body knew.

It makes the 3 Enzyme timer. Called Abraham Iteration. One time right. or 3rd, 5th so on.
and no more.

3 layer of Generic Ruby Drug. No all generic are generic. There are premium index.
Premium position. Errata. Less is more.

10 kind of acute illness. Another 4 is cancer. All treatment by One generic. And 3 branch.

The Bypass is the Destination. There is express route too. 3+1 Generic. Three Enzyme and One Chemistry Cryptography Structure.

This is the 3 Body Timer, and 1 Body Clock. This is Technical Part, also the Hasted Part.
The Protocol Consensus. Original and Final cannot changed.

The safety distance gauge. Hence, this is about finding the Original. Just required two datum.

So Generic Drug is Business, but Chemistry Drug has no business. It seems to many difficult.

The priority and neck is on the Pro-long Grace time. And from them, the common are the Original and Final.

Its a Cryptography Structure Cast Out Structure. This Cast Out Structure is the Original.

From the Studied of Chronicle and Chronography, the Original has two division only.
B.C. ->A.D. ->Post A.D->New B.C. there is only total 8 Division. 8 Pad.

8.1. Channel is fake one. The Grand Piano. All theory is generic, no substitute and one direction. 8+1 is false.

8 Sound Speaker has no bass channel. Grand Piano has no bass. Virtual Bass has no Footage.

It cant transmit out. Its virtual. Who care? Suspicious mind. This called the Footage. 3R vs 4R.

Just call it. You are freedom from sins. Greater than all things, and above all kings.
Near and Far, you cant catch it.

The Moon Rider. Democracy is freedom, from any kind of sins. Its Liberal, to International, and to Global. The 3 Forms of Democracy. Nationalism, Capitalism, Totalitarianism.

All about Human Right Act the Ezra Law as centred. Ezra Law is so called Information Broadcast Law.

Laid out the Foundation of Intelligence Law. The Lent, Loyalty and Royalty. Apart of this is Information Distrust Infringement.

Terrorism control the Other Country is one of the Kind. In which, Against Democracy is Terrorism.

Which is often thought of Anti Semitic, Orthodox Christian Persecution, Anti Natalism.
Those are the Pillar of Democracy. Don't worry about Loyalty, apart from it is Royalty.
Against the Democracy is Religionism. The Socialist.

These two entity works in sync to yield Differential Entity. The Culture, Humanity and Economy Booming. Politic + Religion = Capitalism.

Politic Scapegoat + Religion Think Tank = Capitalism Funding.

Democrat + Marxist = Nationalist

This Nationalist is differential Entity. The New Platform Entity build on Business Misconduction Referendum.

Hence, infringe of Business or Authority Abuse is Rule from this New Platform Entity, the Capitalism Privilege.

Without Capitalism Privilege, this Infringer is received the Justice Penalty at whole.
3 type of Power Authority Abusement, Geography Privilege, Intellectual Privilege, and Heritage Privilege.

All root from Business Misconduction. a.k.a. International Law. And all of this has no black and white. Its about Covenant. International Covenant.

The Meta Law for analogy. This is the Freedom we can enjoy. Justice is kindness, don't abuse it.

It is biased one side, until the day coming. As rule of thumb, Justice is always but it is individual.

Rebounce of evil, is the mistake. This is no about verification, its about Personal Human Right.

As a whole Global Human Right. Run rabbit run. Of course, all is welcome. This is the High Standard we need to target.

Human Right is all right reserved, as always. The better Delay than Postpone. And you can jump across.

There nothing to argue, its Christianity Covenant, and the Universe Law. Let's debate for Marriage, and War for Office.

War is about Capitalism. The platform is Justice. All are welcome. This how the God Ministry Make Money, and Public Ministry Pay Debt.

All are royalty. and loyalty and lent. Its 100% and 100% and 100%. Learn more. The Edge make profits.

So thought Replica Weapon nowadays. The Toxic Weapon. Just leave it for next War. Currently, infringe of this is Fire Lake.

This is not War, this is Pollution. The Bunches of rat. In fact, we are better rat.
Chicken are bunches of rat.

Lets the Righteous voice it. Apart from voicing, we cant do anything other than that.
Lets face the Threat of Mute.

Its a planting of seed, and there is vault there is premium and harvest. Those Make Justice Disorder formed the Toxic Community.

After its individual to Country and Whole World. The One you trust absolutely. Any one without datum belief is dangerous.

This is honesty, and truth. Stop bluffing around. Let's sing. Puppet cannot rule world.
Its about Ethnic and Moral War.

Islam ally is inclined to Ethnic Protection. And Buddhism ally is inclined on Moral Protection. Result oriented and Process oriented.

Now is Forever motto. Label it with Contemporary. You give peanut you get monkey. All are correct, nothing wrong for Justice and Human Right. And Final Justice is Market Pie Share.

Obey the Traffic Protocol is rule of game from banned. That why everybody concerns, the Banned, Boycott and Genocide.

Islam Ally efforts drive into the Heaven, the Matter. And Buddhism Ally efforts drive into the Heaven, the Medium. Gospel Advent + Revelation Oriental.

Two Entity Reaction yield, 3 Differential, the Residue, the Products, and Toxic. It is a Real Number and One Constant.

Its about Quantum Formula, the Iteration Number. Time is Grace. And it is not about Psychology, its Orthogonal Whole Human and Creature.

Grace for you and me. Reject is human right. Hungry man is hurry man. All people bear their own Cross.

Its cant transfer to, even Family. The Direction is clear, from Ancestry to Offspring, no backward.

Deed is transfer from Old Generation to New Generation. No backward. Why, Public Ministry has meet Crisis.

Simply, this is Who moves my Cheese.

The Immaturity this Myth makes Royalism a Criminal Offence. The obstacle is incompletely studied.

When this is truth, there is peace. This required Certain Iteration. One Real Number and One Constant make 9 Solar System.

The Cross Symbol and the Colour hue. Solar System deviate by the Combustion Efficiency.

This is the Heaven Standard. Not too much, not too bad. 22.

The Constant is about 7.2G to 8.5G the Light Speed. When hitting that, it goes into True colour era.

Not too extreme this time. The Islam has to transformed into God Minister. Separating Evil and Righteous, long time.

Called Perfect Islam. No Sigma. All same factory. This is not Holy Spirit. Islam Has no Holy Spirit.

Its 100% Clear stage. When this is Repel Islam, it is Terrorism.

This is the Price to Clear the Next Stage, the Ethnic Protection of Islam ally and Moral Protection of Buddhism ally.

Who rules Heaven is important. Its about the, Configuration of Cross and Colour of the Cross.

Red cross is Islam. The Anti Semitic. Moral is Debating, but Promoted. Semitic Supremacy.

Its the Myth build on Love. And this is Marriage Myth too. This is why most people keep it quite.

Projection into many phase. Computer, OS, Machine, Car. And what enemy can do is Golden Timing. The Crowd Event Attack.

So Mercy and Grace get the Prime. Its 100% pure. Try to reach this Standard of Pure.
The Morality. Is Love.

And Ethnic Protection is Pure. Both are Precious. The Final winner not rule out. But confusing is confucian.

The Adam. Its is one of the 6 minister. No Toxic. Differentiate One Toxic and Two Drug.
Toxic content measured by Hierarchy of bonding.

5 Toxic Rating. Hence, Vaccine can be break in production. The Mild Toxic is Triggering Immunity.

And this immunity is Pasteurization of Cell. What the Generic Drug could failed and Chemistry Drug could failed for Disease Illness.

Disease illness treatment is Herbs. This is the path. Reminder. Start from the Top.
The Ultimate way, the most toxic way. Holy way.

Yes the Herbs. From bottom up, ridiculous. Its about where we heading. Toxic content rating separating Islam ally and Buddhism ally.

Strong toxic, most Righteous people cannot suffer. Herbs way, is the Anti Semitic. But it clear cut the Evil and Righteous in half.

Iteration number is key. My Formula is Max 6R Footage. Quantum 7. There is a myth, due to 6R footage is fake one.

This is the Private Footage. Not Published. What not published is frauding. This is about Published Fee, Official Owner & Public Property. And Locked Fee, Certified Owner & Private Property.

All Privatised Property under one hand. Along the Chronography & Chronicle, the System Constitution is rule by Abraham Islam.

Obey the Abraham Law, is the requirement to make diaspora Heritage, Private Heritage.
Because Privatised Heritage is Free Duty not Growing at all.

Of course that Footage is Toxic, and Holy Place. Moon Rider. Moon is Privatised. No photo published.

5 Constant Rating, and 7 Real Number Rating. 30 Map identified and 5 Privatised Moon
And Clear Stage Mission.

Choose your Own Toxic. Its Cell Pasteurised Methodology, Pentecost Spherical Forms.
Heat Therapy.

Its Paradise 7.2 Knot, or Heaven 7.3 Knot. Knot is Light Years, i.e. Month. Pasteurised Technology using Luminous Light is alternative than Sonar.

Combinative applied can make Many Stem Cells. 70 type of Cells. Good Cells and Bad Cell 35/35. Very Draft.

Hard to judge Good and Bad, Two kinds. These Cell constitute the 14 Body Organ. Who is Mixed, as whole.

Eat would die. The reason is quality control reject is uncertainty. the High Organic, And Advanced Life.

Same thing, not every food is benefit. and some toxic is benefit. Taste is most important.
This comes to Chemistry Cryptography Drug part.

Previous, Vaccine Therapy is triggering body Pasteurization by Selecting the Stem Cell. The Body Immunity Fever mode Triggered.

Enzyme Generic Drug has 3 layers, against the Generic Illness. 3 layers is Body Timer Enzyme against the 10 Kind of Acute Illness.

And the Chemistry Cryptography Drug is against the Chronic Illness. Its to Prolong than Treatment.

But its grey area of what is acute and chronic same time. Hence, Chronic Illness has only 3 type.

Or the 4th One is the Debating. To 3 Body Timer is within the Brain Control. 3 Branch.
Hormone, Carbon, and Poison.

There cannot form up standard. So the Disorder Occurrence is due to Carbon as Subjective. Social Bonding Disorder.

The Nicotine Faulty. And the rootcause is Natal and Spiritual. 50% of Population has this Low Cap.

And the Natal alone is the major Obstacle. This is about the Calcium and Mineral. The Radiation Exposure worsen this Capability.

or Shorten the Paralyses Timeline. So this drug become Demanding. By creating another Body timer.

This makes the Gene become into Homogeneous. The Brain becomes into Bottom Line.
This is only the Platform. Not important.

Chemistry Cryptography Drug is target on shifting the Meta Position. This makes Bald, Erection issue, Blur Eye, Hormone Disorder.

Entire effort is Prevent Paralyses. 2nd target is Cure the Hormone Gender. And 3rd is Cure the Hygienic Orientation.

Hormone Disorder could become Fatigue and Liver Failure. Hygienic Disorder is Meta Disorder. The Stomach Failure.

Kidney is Paralyses, Liver is Retard, Stomach is Deaf. So Those Drug cannot cure, is not Chronic Illness.

Its Mental Illness. There is cure for Mental Illness. Many option and alternative route.
It is to prevent paralyses, Retard and Tinnitus.

There has no guarantee of Detection and Cure Diagnostic. Religion methodology well sought after, but Its Active than Passive.

And the Drug Method still becoming the Dark Market. The Business of these make the Nationalist into Popularism.

And create Un-desire Biomedical Economy Industry. The Issue is not Gene, nor DNA, and Stem Cell either.

Spiritual alone could make these Natalie become more Natalie. Medicine treatment can cure alot, but Economy not sound.

The effort spends on the Medical Machine and Make Wealth. This is undesirable for Human Civilisation.

And This kind of Heritage has lowest graded. Consider nearly Private Footage. And the Amount is enormous and imaginable.

Let those belong Caesar to Caesar, God to God. Let those Dead bury the Dead. Undesirable.

The Missile has eye, no final destination, Rocket has no eye, but final Destination.
Just running to forever. And rocket has limit.

Serve Duty is Forever, Serve Devotion is Numbers. This is separate Ministry and Myth.
Saint serve Ministry, Apostle performs Myth.

Wealthy Man can perform Myth too. Separating Vatican and Catholic. Free Time Apostle and Wealthy Saints.

This is God match.

Christian Medicine – Legacy (Generic Pharmacy) vs New Flagship (Far Medicine)

A. 10.4 Acute Organ Disorder: Timer Correlation (e.g. Migration)

Topical Generic Vitamin, Specific Vitamin + Treatment: Physiology & Technology
Gene RNA: Virus and Tumour Cells
Prime Carrier 1: Chemical Active Vitamin (Specific Mineral Particle)

50 Pair - Acute Organ Disorder a.k.a. Heart Inflammation to Lung Infection Complication

Most Acute Illness is involving Pain and Sudden Death.
Such as, those Required Immediate Surgery Operation.

The Organ Disorder is Body Timer Disorder.
Rootcause:
Group as Cancer Cell: **Blood Cells, Brain Cells, Bone Cells, Teeth Cells**.
Group as Poison Cells: **Lung Cells, Urine Cells, Intestine Cells etc**

Healing Pharmacy:

3 type Enzyme Layer Drug (Intake only), total 6 Prime Enzyme by Chronography Dating of its 6 types of Tempered Mode.

More than 108 Expensive Specific Enzyme,
or 20 type of Available Generic Drug against 50 Acute Organ Disorder.

The Price difference is on the Poison Cell or Cancer Cell, which required more Specific Healing Timing, not too just or too long, worsen to Allergy.

Clinical Trial is to identify the Specific Enzyme to Specific Groups of Ethnic, which is optional and extra Shield.

And Specific Enzyme is against to Particular Illness, and the targeted Organ Cells.

High Allergy is sign of Reject, but it is Personally Hygienic only.
If this occurs, Religion Complementary required.

B. 4.1 Chronic Nerve Failure: Footage Correlation (e.g. Exile)

Natal Issue or Mental Obstacle, in which Natal could lead to Organ Failure. Desirable Risk to be Terminal Illness.
Other side, Mental Obstacle is Curable.

Intake Remedy + Treatment: Mental & Religion
Genealogy DNA: Mental Disorder and Nerve Disorder
Prime Carrier 2: Chemistry Structure Remedy

Nicotine deficiency: Kidney Failure Risk
Either Chronic: **Paralyses** or Curable Symptom: Social Disorder (Personality)
Supplement Drug: Unique Chemistry Structure against, Translating Nervous System
Inner Ear Timer e.g. Diamond Geometric, one of Gold Isotope e.g. Specific Informatic & Inert Particle a.k.a. Fibre Particle (Intake only)

Hormone deficiency: Liver Failure Risk
Either Chronic: **Hearing & Deaf i.e. ENT** or Curable Symptom: Marriage Disorder (Timing)
Supplement Drug: Unique Chemistry Structure against Sensing Nervous System
Sex Gland Timer, e.g. Ruby Geometric, one of Calcium Isotope e.g. Specific Inheritor & Radiant Particle a.k.a. Rice Particle (Intake only)

Carbon deficiency: Stomach Failure Risk
Either Chronic: **Leukemia** or Curable Symptom: Bi-Polar Disorder (Location)
Supplement Drug: Unique Chemistry Structure against Commuting Nervous System
Lymphatic Timer, e.g. Sapphire Geometric, one of Salt Isotope, e.g. Specific Digesting & Energy Particle a.k.a. Mineral Particle (Intake only)

Poison Overtake: Heart Failure Risk
Either Chronic: **Head Damage** or Curable Symptom: Psychology Disorder (Security)
Supplement Drug: Unique Chemistry Structure against Central Nervous System
Brain Timer, e.g. Pearl Geometric, one of Rubber Isotope, e.g. Specific Gum & Malt Particle a.k.a. Glucose Particle (Intake only)

C. 5.0 Cancer Immune Defect: Chronography Correlation (e.g. Retirement)

Injection & Topical, the Informatic Vaccine - Treatment: Vaccine Herbs + Pasteurisation & Nurtured
Genetic mDNA: Organ Failure and Cancer
Prime Carrier 3: Enzyme Cryptography Vaccine

Pasteurised Technology using Luminous Light is alternative than Sonar.

Combinative applied can make Many Stem Cells.

Commentary

5 Rating of Vaccine, but grouped as one Unity entity. 70 type of Cells. Good Cells and Bad Cell 35/35. Very Draft. Hard to judge Good and Bad, Two kinds. These Cell constitute the 14 Body Organ. Who is Mixed, as whole. Eat would die. The reason is quality control reject is uncertainty. The High Organic, And Advanced Life. Same thing, not every food is benefit. and some toxic is benefit. Taste is most important. This comes to Chemistry Cryptography Drug part. Previous, Vaccine Therapy is triggering body Pasteurization by Selecting the Stem Cell. The Body Immunity Fever mode may Triggered.

Y551. Christian Medicine XIII: Castle in the Sky the New Grounded for De-Viral (Journal)

Patch: Correlation Schism per Capital Clan

De-Viral : Patch per Ecumenical Judification Constitutions

Ecumenical Judification Constitutions : De-Viral + Patch

*The Concept is to Change the Foundation Support into Pillar Support. Hence the Foundation Schism become into Correlation Patch, and the Patched Ecumenical Constitutions become into De-viral Version.

*The Patch is Parametric & Genetic Coating. And only a Fully Patch Parametric, can permitted De-Viral, in which the Outer Coating is Join-off.

(Credit to "Square Tan Fang Zhen", Foon Yew Orchestra Fellow)

Y525. Christian Medicine XI: Off Duty Machine Framework, Navigation, Metrology, Biomedical (Journal)

I. Class A1 Scheme, Data Mark: Computer, Route (Biomedical, Industrial Product)

A Class, the First Class: **Modular to Universal, Biomedical Framework, Route of Chemical, Chemistry, Organic, Air, Fluid, Smoke to Dust not the least.**

A Class: Progressive Weighted, Holy & Emotional, Piano
1R Len Footprint, 8R Spiritual Footage i.e. Remastered

II. Class C Scheme, Kelvin Mark: Laboratory, Len (Metrology, Enterprise Product)

B Class the Guarantee Class: **Quart Tempered ->Music the Gauging Instrument, Dating Identification**
E Class the Inaugural Class: **Diode Annealed ->Camera the Thermal Device, Calligraphy Prevention**
D Class, the VIP Class: **Calcium Pasteurised ->Plotter the Magnetic Commuting Machine, Metrology Security**

B Class: Light Touch, Merry & Fun, Keyboard
2R Len Footprint, 5R Modulated Footage i.e. Echo

E Class: Retouch, Milky & Dummy, Flute
4R Len Footprint, 9R Regulated Footage i.e. Theatre

D Class: Final Touch, Graces & Duty, Guitar
5R Len Footprint, 10R Tuned Footage i.e. Surround

III. Class F4 Scheme, Hall Mark: Music, Mic (Navigation, Consumer Product)

F Class the Gone Case: **Silicon Fabrication, Semiconductivity Transducer: Calculation**
C Class the Conceded: **Germanium Manufacturing, Superconductivity Sensor: Navigation**

F Class: Weight Expression, Glory & Impressive, Acoustic
3R Len Footprint, 6R Toned Footage, i.e. Stereo

C Class: After Touch, Plainly & Luxury, Cello
2R Len Footprint, 7R Dynamic Footage i.e. Dolby

Errata 20Jan2023

Y578. Christian Medicine XXIX: Those High Meta Capita
Natalie Royal Christian Army (Journal)

I. **Trojan Host (GER)/Net Bus** (RUS) EMF, Parametric Pentecost Patches i.e. Correlation to Genocide or Footprint/Sky
8 Beats Soul (White)->16 Beats Sambals (Red)/1/3 Beats Bossa Nova (Pink) (Biblical Identity, Book of Life, Olive Nativity)
UN (SG), *Security Trade of Oriental*
Islam (Islam Noel the End of the World): Long Keris II (Global Class), Meta Stellar Head Sheppard Dog - Oriental

II. **Rabbit/Fox IR**, Geothermal Blueprint Projection i.e. Eschatology Calendar/Moon
Carrie Tither->Carrie Commuting (Personal Cryptograph->High Metric Cryptography)
NATO (SG's RUS), *Security Wage Adventist*
Christian: Atonement Cross Meta Jesus - Adventist

III. **Kings/Queens** UV, Geothermal Blueprint i.e. Ecumenical/Mar
Holy Spirit->Stellar Head (Credential Copyright->Fashion Heritage)
WWF (US), *Communication Feedback of Promised Land*
Buddhism the West: Jerusalem Timezone Meta the Deer – Promised Land (Earth Village Route)

IV. **Unicorn/Transformer** ESD, Motorised Metallurgy Power Value i.e. Judification/Jupiter
Nerve Toxic->Hue Depth (Dust Address->Quantum Timezone)
KMT (MY), *Live Communication of Utopia*
Vatican: Redemption Cross II Meta Jesuit - Utopia

V. **Zion the Testimoners/Scout** ESD, i.e. Etymology/Olive (Canaan Isle), Asteroid (Coral Isle), Comet (Satellite Isle), Supernova (Organism i.e. Ether Isle)
Nerve Maturity->Ageing Security (Marriage Meta Tither->True Love or False Love Duty the Misconduction of Marriage)
NASA (MY's HK), *Marriage Generations of Renaissance Dead End Mileage*
Buddhism the East: Moscow Timezone Meta the Monalisa – Jupiter (Hell Route)
High Metric Time, Spiritual Food vs Titus Food i.e. Token Food
Islam Renaissance (Islam Castle in the Sky): Short Keris (Federal), Meta Antichrist – Renaissance

VI. **Gabriel/Lilith** UV, Descriptor the 5per Lens e.g. Prism/Ether Mar
Pentecost->Holy See (Algorithm Milestone->Aggregate Milestone)
WHO (US's AU), Heaven with True Love or False Love Duty Route

Buddhism the Light: Bethlehem Timezone Meta the Messi – Solar 7th (Fire Lake Route)

Disruption the Germany Trojan Host for Eliminating the High Security Vulnerability of Nativity of Chinese in Singapore Alternative the Russia Net Bus.

Y268. Genocide Insight: Diamond is Forever (Forum)

The Religion Reformation is top urgency. Its has to be justified. Not too quick. Ethnic tells more. Its boxing time. Present is always benefit.

When schism become equilibrium it become one body and neutralised. From Democrat Socialist to Republican Socialist. Ok, it have to be always move to avoid Republicanised.

Progressive not instantaneous works. Basket Ball vs Football. African, Germanic vs Semitic, Chinese. No matter how, it has been plotted.

Depend how justice define. Flagged vs Framework. There are Communist and Marxism Socialist. Two are oppose each other.

For God kingdom, it has to be Flagged. It is about as large as Exodus. So you say what is justice? Its Individual. and we have to address Justice.

For Holy Spirit is Hub, the Justice is Harp. And Harp is Marxism Socialist. and Communist Justice is Bowing instead of Strumming.

Social Focus vs Material Focus. And this is China Regime. The Marxism and Communist, two entity. Marxism trace back to Soviet Union. and Mao Zhe Dong.

Alot Disguised. Its a Paradox. "The Dream of the Red Chamber" Sheep and Goat... All are Christian. Its about Active and Passive Salvation.

Meant, All Semitic are Nature Borned Christian. Suffer compensate vs Salvation compensate. The different is here, the Tangible and Non Tangible.

And this mean Marxism pro to Germanic, and Communist pro to Semitic. This proof China is Marxism Dominated. And the War Against China is apparently.

Clear Path... Its now Federation Russia. Republican Socialist is Federation. Democrat is Islamic. Republican is Buddhism, and Marxism is Christianity.

Its eyebrow fire... To avoid all kind of disaster, we have to fight with the Unidentified Object and Evil. Lets make it peace, this time is Mafia vs Monarchy.

Called Royalism, e.g. Whitehouse Think tank. Semitic is Mafia inclined. Very funny... Clap clap clap... Its Naked..

So, its about Baptism, my mother say. Force Repentance is a Criminal. Terrorism.. Yes, Terrorism cannot be whiten. This is Love..

Where is my grape? Its about Rare Earth Economy, Repentance become a worship. This is all begin with Brexit.

Its a change of game from Goat to Sheep. The Church Reformation. And we know there is biased. The Biased of Evil toward Semitic.

So this is how the Justice born. Semitic Law is the Most stringent Law. The Imperialism. This Law is experimental research for more than million of year in each Civilisation e.g. Ice Age, Jurassic etc.

And the Gospel Act is experimental research for more and less 5000 years. Rumour called Moses Ark. And this is Climate Protocol. Best Version.

To change from Imperialism to Marxism might conflict to Climate Protocol. After all, its about Climate, and we shall have abundant of Prosperity. And Marxism Socialist is Condemned for abolishment of Colony or Slave.

Especially of the A.I., Robotic and Automation. The Anti Semitic Marxism, Buddhism. Called it Taliban. Orthodox Christianity is Truely Anti Semitic. That is also the Disruption of Digital Economy.

What the next move? For Climate Protocol, we cannot Tolerated Marxism expanding. But we lose to the Big Trend.. This world has to be Homogenous Unity.

This is the United Nation Policy. The Democrat Socialist, building the Promised Land. Together with Democracy Nationalist.

After all, mathematically mistake is Satanic. China Marxism Socialist shall Co-Exist Each Other with Taiwan Democracy Nationalist. One land two system. Even the Flag has down, the Law will not be perished.

Its about Gross National Product with/without per capita. It can't live without auto mechanism to equilibrium and optimisation. This is the Monitoring system i.e. Auditing.

Its about Population Genocide. Like wise, EU and UK, RUS and US. The total 6 automation Mode, and total 6 Element of Algorithm. To make the Optimised Result. Can no one less.

This make a Harp curve. This Harmony is Perpetual, any disruption is temporary. Its a number. The 14 Generation. The Harmony the Power will not fade. This is because it can only accumulated but not decrease.

And there is begin and there is closing. Assurance is it will not growth or decay. But Mutation itself. Aftermath is clustering everywhere.

The Earth Village. Well, its connected Majority to Minority. For sure, it wont explode or decay but mutate. This is called Germs. It will not growth at all.

Instead it exhausting. Back to the topic. Stop by the 6 Mode and 6 Element of Politic Ideology. No any Politic Ideology cannot be abolished.

And the Harmony Curve will not changed and maintenance same shape due to Ranking. Its a wasting of resource trying to disruption the harmony 6s.

Its life. Every life has three forms, Solid, Gaseus and Liquid. Trying to disruption is waste, and you will not make it empty.

And the Sign of Harp is everywhere same. Once again, every life has ranking and are precious. Trying to Change the Harmony, its your personal success, but our disgrace.

Just wake up. That is my diamond. Diamond is forever. Of course, First is Last, Last is First.

So?? Blame your wings.

Politic Insight

Republican Catholic ISIS Buddhism
Marxism Orthodox Taliban Islam
Nationalist Presbyterian Hinduism
Fasci Cult a.k.a. Nazi Organised Syndicate | Qing Syndicate

Democracy Baptist Protestant
Communist Episcopal Reformed
Democrat Charismatic Aqueda Pentecostal
Nazi Cult | Mafia

Errata 22Aug2022

Copyright (C) 2022, Ryan Lai Hin Wai, All right reserved.

Volume 3: Encyclopedia for Advanced Christian Learner, by Footage, Footprint, Calligraphy, and Carrier.

Newbies or Dead End

Messi God Kingdom Focus: From Renaissance Beta to Oriental Renaissance

Christian Finance: Economic Methodology to Quantum Treasure
Christian Education: Theology
Biblical Application: Doctrinal Training
Puritan Music: Church Music
Social Engineering: Social Scamming

Y531. Christian Finance S: Tax Legislation Framework, the Dismiss from Preliminative, Dating to Allergy (Review)

A. Legislation (Aged), Food Bill Scheme (Machine)
*Footprint Suit, i.e. Preliminative Grant Protocol, Carbon Tax
e.g. Craftsmanship, Hall Mark, Real Value i.e. R Mark, Kelvin Mark, Data
Mark (Cryptography Treasure Ministry, the Dramatic Journey of Seeking)*

i. White Sea, Strait, Sea Food: Dollar (Colonel) 将军 vs 诸葛亮
ii. Yellow Sea, Deep, Salted: Won (Doctor) 华佗 vs 民医
iii. Red Sea, Strait, Diamond: Bucks (Engineer) 太保 vs 金刚
iv. Yellow River, Deep, Pearl Food: Sterling (President) 皇帝 vs 朱太子
v. Gland Sea a.k.a. Dead Sea, Strait, Coral: Yuan (Scientist) 大臣 vs 孙策
vi. White River, Strait, Stellar Organic: Pound (Lawyer) 状元 vs 孔子

B. Commuting (Colour Card Credit), License Fare Suit (Enclosure)
*Meta Clan i.e. Allergy Whistle Policy, Real Value, Stellar Class, Casting by
Alcohol: i. Sake Fruity Yeast ii) Cocktail Fruity Brew iii) Israelite Whiskey iv)
Hebrew Whiskey v) Wine vi) Beer (Economy Treasure Ministry, the Legislation
Milestone to Judification)*

i. George Town (CUV/ESV/NIV)(White): Sake or Dairy 22.5 deg = Only
Class **A1 Scheme, Union**, (Interposed) Chronography Era, *Sea Route
become Duty Locked, **Space/Castle** 食*
ii. China Town (CSB/KJV)(Gland): Cocktail -22.5 deg = Only Class **C
Scheme, International**, *Navigation Era, Economy Path become Straight, Free
Trade/Harbour e.g. **Intelligence Street** 住*
iii. Funky Town (CCB/NKJV)(Green): Wine 180+22.5 deg = Only Class **F4
Scheme** (Islam Ally), **Federation**, Tither Era, *Protocol Footage become
Footprint, Weather Control/Land Mark e.g. **Cabbed Car** 衣*
iv. Christ Town (Hebrew/Tyndale)(Red): Beer or Chocolate 180-22.5 deg =
Only **Class A1** Scheme (Buddhism Ally), **Federals**, *Quantum Era, Space
Track become Autopilot, Satellite Modular Assembly below the Ground Tunnel.
e.g. **Token Jukebox** 行*

C. Security (Route), Tuition Fee Gate (Computer)
*Footage Zone i.e. Dating Zone Treaty, Fruit Buffer e.g. 1) Anti God, Yeast-
>Diamond 2) Anti Semitic, Brew->Coral 3) Anti Chinese, Cultured->Pearl
(Conjugating into Christian Treasure Ministry, the Chronicle Final Touch)*

i. Silk Road->Olive Road, Rolling Boat (Pilgrim), Diamond-> Pineapple
(Einstein)(+1min)(Roller) 纯文艺 (大姨妈)
Canyon Road->Milestone Road, Judi Force (Easter Day), Gold-> Glucose
(Stellar)(+6min)(Counter) 柏拉图 (男生)

ii. Great China Wall->Mile End Road, Prison (Pentecost Day), Pearl-> Durian (Newton)(-6min)(Real Made) 割礼派 (女生)
Israel Wall->Fig Tree Road, Congress (Christmas the Nativity), Silicon-> Mango Fiber (Quantum)(+5min)(Carbon) 博爱 (复刻派)

iii. Berlin Wall->Economy District, Resort (Christmas the Bethlehem), Coral-> Watermelon (Scalar)(-5min)(Pollution) 真爱 (印象派)
Schism Road->Island Area best of Pentagon the 55th, Church 三岔口 (Passover Day), Calcium-> Dairy (Modular)(-1min)(Plug and Play) 法利赛 (安息日)

Y539. Christian Finance V: Economic Blueprint (Industrial Version)(Review)

A. Combustion Reaction->Heritage->Royalty->Sterilisation Value->Jeopardy Fee (Seeking Tempered Products)
What, Cryptography: Meta->Biblical Translation & Theology Pillar
Industrial Holistic Framework Treaty

B. Organism Exchange->Food->Loyalty->Stellalisation Value->Holysee Charge (Seeking 5.2 Bridge)
Why, Mileage: Pentecostal->Canonical Commentary & Theology Platform
Banking Legislation Policy

C. Solar Activities->Energy->Fare->Stellar Value->Dust the Geology Wage (True Colour Seeking)
Who, Carrier: Quantum->Scripture & Theology Foundation
University Duty Protocol i.e. Local & Foreign Pillar Coring

D. Fusion Mechanism->Intellectual->Lent->Crystallisation Value->Footage Segment (Cornerstone Seeking)
When, Milestone: Parametric->Church Security & Theology Legacy
Canon of Bible Natalie Congress

Y554. Christian Finance Y: The Banking Mistake Three Mode (Review)

I. Premier Banking Myth: Quantum Number is Credit in Advanced the Risk Accounting. Degrading of Climate Change Kelvin Mark as well as Human Heritage e.g. Genealogy or Biblical Treasure, Criminal Blueprint, Carrie Election of Individual makes Credit Card Kick Out. The Humanity Crime getting Escalating or Lift up Platform when Kelvin Mark Error Happens, in Rush Hour. The Time Metric Computational Formula Mistake, made Series of Aftermath. The Replicating of this is no more loops but Perceive-ness Choice of Community Leader to least bonding.

II. Caesar Banking Myth: Metallurgy analogy the Paper Scissor Stone, the Fallacy. The Meta Scaled is the Universal Constant, the Event Calendar Division, in terms of Metric, Meta, Tither, Cryptography, Calligraphy, Colour Hue, conjugating as Light Speed Footage, i.e. Holoscope Footage. The Metallurgy End Product Treatment Evolution Divisional Timeline make the Fallacy into Scamming of Intellectual exchange to Heritage, and Poverty Class lead into Fashion Class, the Strategic Endervour attract Fallen of Duty of Job and Economy Treasure into wrong hands, i.e. Caesar. This totally a Trick. The Bible tells us, Each Commitment has their Bonds, and this is not Credit Gain in Advanced, but Global Class Economy Maturity Milestone.

III. Banking Schism the Security & Financial Products Myth: The Value of Security is based on the Time Saver Metric Standard, and this link-up to the Security Products those Electronics Thermal Machine, Device and Instrument and Financial Products Risk Forecast Claimed. The Conjugates of these makes the Value of Security in Gross Deficit Trade Zone which is also the Economy Treasure in Schism Road of Christian Army the Salvation Devotions Day by Days. Hence, the compromised the either goes e.g. Security Product Stalled, or Financial Products Misalignment Carrier Axis and Meta Clock the Hygienic Clock, to Economy Loss Series Aftermath as Wholly Humanity Crime, the Primary initiative of Salvation of Christian Army widely sought after.

IV. Banking the Currency Trade Zone Myth: The Gross Trade Zone Deficit, are the Straight Path of Economy Time Zone. This Time Zone has the Best Education Bonding to the Metric Gain of All Phase of Industrial Framework. Hence, the Currency of all this kind contributing the Currency Framework based entirely on the Industrial and Medicine Framework.

Y446. Christian Education XXIII: Church Organisation & Superstars (Post)

A. (Second Resort), Comet x 1 out of 100: Primary Pearl colour, Dots Forms i.e. Asteroid with High Voltage Star Dust.
e.g. Korea (Babel Tower - Anti Tsunami to End World Backup Plan) – **Utopia I**
Minor Prophet to Major Prophet (Dice vs Diamond)

B. (Last Resort), Virgin Habitat Earth x 1.5: Primary Gold Colour, Planetary Forms i.e. Meta Energy Core to Quantum Energy Shield
e.g. Singapore (Canyon Road - Utopia Dream and Utopia Trial) – **Promised Land**
Gentile to Ace (Olive vs Fig)

C. Supernova Planets x 1: Primary Sapphire colour, Pentecost Spherical Forms with Many Galaxies.
e.g. China (Great Wall of China - Disaster Trial) – **Oriental I**
Scapegoat to Apostle (White Light vs Chromatic Light)

D. Supernova Planets x 1: Primary Jade colour, Meta Spherical Forms with Many Solar Systems.
e.g. United States (Berlin Wall - Pandemic Trial) – **Oriental II**
Antichrist to Disciple (Low Voltage Salt vs High Voltage Salt)

E. (First Resort), Solar Planet x 8.5: Quantum colour 9 Kind, Fish & Chopstick Forms Planet (Unstable but Primitive of Advanced Organics) i.e. The Seven Fish Independent Knot Formation.
e.g. United Kingdom (Silk Road - Addressing & Preaching Mission to World Nine Continent a.k.a. Big Nine Annealed Zone) - **Advent**
Low Cards to Royalflush (Timber vs Wood)

F. Comet x 8: Ruby colour, Star Cube Forms i.e. Asteroid with Star Dust Collector.
e.g. Israel (Jerusalem Wall - Religion War) – **Utopia II**
Nun to Saint (Fur vs Silk)

Y478. Christian Education XXV: The Understanding of Cult by Moses Law (Post)

The First Law of Moses is the Foundation for Beginner. And this Law should not be compromised or whole System Collapse.

If the whole System Doesn't Collapse, it is linked to other Root instead.

And this Root is with the Son of God, the one who has the Son has God and life. The one denied has nothing, and rejected by Perpetual Autopilot.

Hence, this is the example of current Church Crisis and World Government Crisis the Charismatic Wave Campaign Number 3.

Y587. Christian Education XXXIV: Universal Constant and Pi Number Easter (Post)

Pi Number
Rolls Number
3.14156
Non-Discreet Footprint Universal Constant in Applied Physic Dimensionless Function.
e.g. Lambda Ray

Experimental determined the Dimensionless Scaled Boundary Datum.
Property Value.

The Reynold Number of 2 phase laminar to turbulent make the Property value closure.

This required Wind Mill test in Zero Gravity.

Stellar Dust Cryptography Experiment

to Get the Realism Cryptography to determine the Metrology in Whole Universe Timeline.
Calendar of End time.

Meta Story Hybrid with Brute Force Economy Science to get Perfection Meta as wholly Final Result.

Economy Treasure in All Parallel World to 7th Solar Final Heaven.
Not the Upside down Heaven, not the Hell liked.

Holy Spirit, cautious, could be understood as Biblical Community Ranking, it is a Quantised as a **Regulator's Indication**, in which to make equilibrium balance and robust conjugating calibration. The Real Number Score of Equilibrium Index and Calibration Index.

e.g. Union Labour (Nazism, God Will) to Generic Standard (Marxism, God Grace), International Contemporary (Fascism, Public Ministry) a.k.a. **Quantum Clock (English Level, Righteous the Original), 2nd Pilgrim is Coating only, it is Fade off easily.**

Hence, **Per Capita Milestone:** Lambda, Lion, Horse, Dragon, Epsilon, Sigma - Graded Defect

Commuting to/from 6 Chronicle Timeline, the Methodology by Teleport

I. Future (Heaven/Hell Route i.e. Third World)
Cloud i.e. Peninsular a.k.a. Canaan Land (High Capita, Natalie): Epsilon (Horse Offspring), Sigma (Lion Offspring) (Conversion to Cloud by Rocket, Metrology calibration)
- Mars/Deep Sea
Rocket back to Isle

II. Present (Adventist/Fire Lake Route i.e. Dark Age)
Dust i.e. Coral Isle a.k.a. Jordan River of Salted (Med Capita, Intellect): Horse (Unicorn), Dragon (Mafia) (Conversion to Dust by Car, Cryptography calibration)
- Moon/Pilgrim Land
Car back to future

III. Past (Utopia/Renaissance Route i.e. First World)
Organic i.e. Isle a.k.a. Mining of Valuable Jewellery, New Jerusalem the Universe Gross Capital City (Low Capita, Maverick): Lambda (Dragon Offspring), Lion (Sheppard Dog) (Conversion to Organic by Ship/Air Craft, Chronography calibration)
- Outer Space/Sky High
Ship departure to the Present

*Those Belong to Love, in Couple or remain as Single,
e.g. Titus (Dramatic alone), Galatians (Dinner Marriage, and Corinthians (Pluto acceptance) are not belong to this Groups the Threat and Vulnerably to become Low Capita Maverick, i.e. Trojan Horse Probing, Duty Ransom, False Accuser Lawsuit, etc.

The usual way of creating Erotic Defect by Mind Poison at Prime Closure and add on the Toxic channel path the Perfect Hygience of 1% tolerance.

Y589. Christian Education XXXVI: Application of Moses Law (Post)

I. Moses Dating: called True Love to Marriage Love.
Standard of Heaven required 5 closure from 5 Dating lapsed of time.

II. Moses Patch: Correlation with quota, cannot too many correlation

III. Moses Number the Iterative Number: e.g. Social Bonding Axis
e.g. Moses 8: Theoretical, Moses 9: Experimental.

IV. Covenant of Law: The Universe Law of Automatic Calibre and
   Execution.
10 Law of Moses for any simulated Model. e.g. Climate, Social, Technology,
   Food

3 or minimal 2 closure per capita, the **Biblical Identity**

Goat (Anointed, Gift), Scapegoat: Over Preliminative

Y590. Christian Education XXXVII: Pillar element of Christianity to Final Christian Dating (Post)

Love Faith Hope Works Justice - the **Pillar element of Christianity**, Alternated or Extra

The Faith is just the Tither of Meta, Arts Meta Value in Currency. Price of Faith. Soul Ranking, Duty Ranking. Heritage ranking, Recognition. Credential
Biblical Meta Story method or Scientific training
The False Bonding
Low Carrier tither e.g. non Semitic. those non credential is disobey the law of war.

Economy loss due to **poverty of fraud heritage** of non tax i.e. running tax
False identity, identity thief, the Path Way to Low Capita Maverick

Love Faith Hope Works Justice 5 Standard of Heave send you to Mars.
become Major Prophet of Biblical in Heaven.
Utopia Nativity of Jerusalem Citizen High capita
Promised Land Economy Treasure the Crime Disruption Treasure

Adventist Heaven, Escort of Carrier of All Ethnic those belong to God the Semitic to the Eternality of Eden Garden the Original.

Y591. Christian Education XXXVIII: Equipping of Next Noel the Generic Christian (Post)

Assurance of Victory: Fight against the Evil.

a. Forgiveness by 777 against the Alternate Spirit the Extreamist Exodus Law

b. Patience by 101 variety, against the Youth Spirit the Low Capita. Genesis Law the Apple cannot once at all.

c. Righteous by 50 the limited calibre of ownself, against the False Spirit the Marriage duty Misconduction. Without Credential. Lead to Sabotage Victim Satan.
Leviticus Law.

Anabaptism has Route to Fallacy
Pilgrim is not important. instead of that. Account of bank in church important, similarity has alot. Early Bird Concept will never changed. Maturity of Investment is next day. Analogy to True Love in Corinthians, the Rainbow Bridge Salvation Theology.

Key of Core Technology, the 4 Medicine Engine

a. Life Organism Activity: Hall Mark (Imaginary, Projection i.e. Reflection Image), Complex Number (Derivative Constant, the Aggregates Meta a.k.a. Function)

b. Combustion Reaction: Kelvin Mark (Future), Real Number (2 Score Mark Risk Analysis, Formula, Latin A,B,C, Downline Generations)

c. Solar Electric Mechanism: Data Mark (Past Time), Pure Number (Integer Counts the Audited Index, Roman I, II, III, Mapping Series)

d. Nuclear Fusion: Gravity Mark (Present), Natural Number (Constant Data, Greek Number, Random Rolls Sequence 24per)

Y592. Christian Finance: Actuary Science, the Marriage & Career & Social Costing Value Framework (Review)

Meta Commuting Loading: Dust Interval->The Harbour, Quantum Real Value, Personal Basis Packet

Quantum Tither Maturity: Demography Interval->Tertiary Education, Property Value
Marriage inclined God Ministry Duty Interval: [Personal Basis Packet] [Embedded Carrier] [Property Value] = Stacking of Real Value

i. Titus, Quartet Duty (Foundation) for Ego Self Seeking Image (inert): Stacking of Real Value = Alpha, Beta, 11th, Inaugural, Greek Rolls – Remastered (High Value Love vs Certified True Love), Epidemic Genocide vs Pandemic Jihad Vulnerable

ii. Galatians, Duty free (Business) for Technology (interpose): Stacking of Real Value = A, B, C, Latin Generations – Offspring (Family Heritage vs Personal Innovation), Terrorism vs Earthquake Vulnerable
*Those who has Love has Eternal Life, and those has not found love has not Eternal life.
But if you are tempted from love, you can find Eternal life through existence Preliminative Platform to Jesus or Those Saints. – Paul Epistles

iii. Corinthians, Duty Auto (Military) for Broken Healing (interpose): Stacking of Real Value = Do re mi, Roman Series – Checkmate (6 Parallel Own Capita Image) (Pentecostal Love vs Orthogonal Love), Tsunami vs Nuclear Vulnerable
Parallel Trojan Host: Capita Image in 666=294 Lock Eden Garden Footage Milestone i.e. 294 Biblical Nativity Era.
Destruction Engineering: Express Fabricated Arsenal i.e. Weapon House

A. **Devil/Joshua (Multi National Foundation): Alternated Core Holy Spirit** (Stellar Populated)(Ceramic Skin, Tither Gentile)(Herald)
1 Dating (Deep Sea, Dust), Stevenburg & Ancient Dragon, (Adventist Express Heaven) – (Unplugged) 3G/6G GSM/Universal Chipset Engine Instrument (Sonic Radar, Anti Mis-Orbital Object Accident cum With Gas Meter Metrology Vision Control)(Quantum Car mounting Weapon, Human Behaviour Control the Volume Control 24 Greek Physics Constant to Quantum Field of 24per Isle Configuration Map), Oriental Promised Land (Canaan Peninsular)->Adventist True God Heaven (**6th Global Class Final Boosting, MY**) (Moses Open Red Sea, Fountain Harbour Sentosa Casino)(5D Women Made Manual Tuning)
Olive Road – Silk Road, Pilgrim Castle – (Black Hole Route), Biblical Villain i.e. 666 Whitelist Sigma, High Rank Meta = 22 Meta Capita, Final Church, Lock 3 (5 Lightyears, Original), Original Loop (Philemon, i.e. Jordan the African World Bank Bond House), ISIS Nazi Stakeholder Whitelist (Sleep Dragon Terrorism, Japan Imperial Mafia)
CSB, ASV (Corinthians), King James i.e. Apollo (Space & Medicine Agency i.e. Licenses) (Semitic Industrial Medicine Linked Agency)

B. **False Christ the Beast/Chris (Global Economic Congress): Extra Core Holy Spirit** (Nominal Populated)(Pentecost, Fundamentalist Natalie)(Episcopal)
Nil (Land, Organic), Christian & Natalie Maverick, Herald Renaissance Heaven – (Standalone) 3.5G/7G WCDMA/Remote Control Device – Herald Renaissance the Original Heaven (**1st Village Spiritual, UK**) (Mafia Organised Fasci Stella Head 19th Candidate God Father, Car Park Token City Square City) (Formation Satellites Lock Weapon, Anti Tsunami)(Quantum, Satellite Lock Sea of Lower Reynold for Immediate Turbulent i.e. Non Liquid Stickiness, Tsunami)(4D Man Made Manual Configuration)
Canyon Road – Milestone Road, Judi Armed Force (Hell Route), Sea King/Queen i.e. Etymology (Colony), Low Rank Meta = 20 Meta Capita, Final Foundation (Mafia Holiday Plaza), Lock 10 (5 Lightyears, Parallel), Parallel Loop (Corinthians i.e. Buckingham Chancellor the Final Judger), Qing Organised Stakeholder Blacklist (Black Dragon, Organised, Escort Penthouse, Colonel)
CNVB, ESV, Queen Nazareth i.e. Wisery (Music & Property Agency, Professional)(Natalie Industrial Medicine Linked Agency)

C. **Satan/Nazareth (Universal Sky Ape): Incapability Holy Spirit** (No Heritage)(Inked Skin, Fundamentalist Intellect)(Pentecostal)
3 Dating (Sky, Organic), Jacob & Lilith, New Nativity the Oriental Heaven (Unplugged) 1G/5.5G/High Voltage/Magnetic Stone (Ionizer, Anti Ether Protein Organism Medium Image Distortion to Suicide, the Lion Body Human Face)(Quantum Toxic Gas Weapon) – Oriental Renaissance->Oriental Jerusalem the Inaugural Renaissance Heaven (**5th Multi National Realism, US**) (10D Lord Made Automated Breakable Off)
Great China Wall – Mile End Road, Airport Weather Tower (Earth Village Route), Heavenly King/Queen i.e. New Nativity, New Olive or Bloomberg Meta = 6 Meta Capita, Final Clan (Final Exodus, Pilgrim Place), Lock 2 (First 5 Lightyears, Alpha Sunday a.k.a. 1st Day the Golden Day), Golden Loop (Jude i.e. Ancient Dragon, Western Security Bank), Nazi Zion Thinktank Whitelist (White Dragon, the Nazi High Rank Academy)
CUV, KJV Translation (Titus), Junior King James, i.e. George Washington (Monarchy Royalist), Desperado Ego vs CNVB (Revelation), Inaugural James 7th, (Public Executive Agency, i.e. Licenses)(Semitic Investment Bank Linked)

D. **Serpent/James (International Land Remote): Young Holy Spirit** (Maverick)(Orthogonal, Christian Sheep)(Fundamentalist)
4 Dating (Moon, Cloud), Abraham & Sarah, Inaugural Utopia the Final Heaven (**2nd International Parallel World, RUS**) (Standalone) 4G/8G LTE/USB (Deep Sea Tunnel, Anti Word Prison)(Quantum Informatic Disease Code Weapon)(3D Queen Made Autopilot) – Jupiter
Israel Wall, Fig Tree Road, Bethlehem Town (Dead End Mileage Route), Fallen Angel i.e. Ecumenical Dusk (Trojan Horse Remote), Fig Tree Meta = 6 Meta Capita, Final Metropolis (New Jerusalem Christ Town Tun Aminah, IT Marketplace), Lock 6 (Last 5 Lightyears, Inaugural Black Friday Day a.k.a. 31th Day), Friday Loop (Galatians i.e. Unicorns), Nazi Zion Scapegoat Whitelist (White Dragon, the Pentagon, Christian Organisation, the Crab Machine Sky Army)
Hebrew Tyndale Translation, Junior Queen Nazareth, i.e. Abraham Lincoln (Politic Founder)(Royal Ministry Foundation, i.e. Heritage Legacy)(Natalie Investment Bank Linked)

E. **Man of Sins/Jesuit (Global Secret Garden): Graded Core Holy Spirit** (Beaten)(Ashed Skin, Christian Goat)(Catholic)
2 Dating (Strait, Dust), Noel & James, Eden Garden the Renaissance Milestone Heaven (**4th Nation Wide Authentic, AU**) (Unplugged) 4.5G/9G (2D King Made, Pilot-run, Standard or Generic or A-Z) Wifi/NTSC (High Hue Supernova, Anti Nuclear)(Quantum Dilated Shield Weapon) – Utopia
Berlin Wall, Holland Road, Economy Belt (Hell Route), Underground Mafia i.e. Eschatology Chronicle Emperor, Low Index Meta = 200 Meta Capita, Final Community of Advent (Apostle Democrat Tournament for Final Judification, Christian Organisation, Fasci Communist the China Opposition), Lock 1 (5 Lightyears), Alpha Loop (Hebrew, Tiananmen Square), Fasci UN Mafia Thinktank Blacklist (Dark Dragon, i.e. Underground Mafia) CCB, NKJV Translation, New King James i.e. Pineapple Universal Modular Machine (Liberal Judi Congress i.e. Eschatology Calendar)(Semitic Security Bank Linked)

F. **False Prophets/Messi (Nation Metro Runway) or Santa Claus: Gentile** (Animal Premier)(Holy See, Tither Lamb the Anointed Cultivated)(Vatican)
5 Dating (Mars, Cloud), Adam & Eve, Original Eden Garden, Beta Utopia Heaven (**3rd Universal Dream, SG**) (Standalone) 5G/10G (1D God Made Automatic on/off) Bluetooth/Blue-ray (Germanium, Anti Time Stalled Raping)(Quantum Hormones Weapon) – Solar 7th
Schism Road, Steven Road, Adam Road (Fire Lake Route, i.e. Age Lock I<>II<>I)(Fire Lake Route), Celebrity, i.e. Adventist Meta (Word Prison), High Index Meta = 200 Meta Capita, Final 19th Stellar Head Country (George Town Penang liked Stir Fly), Look 7 (5 Lightyears) Omega Inaugural Loop (Titus i.e. Holiness Tither, Swiss Bank Security Compensation Packet, New Chinese Reunion Security Bank, New Whitehouse), Fasci UN Scapegoat Whitelist (Flying Dragon i.e. Freelance Mafia)
NIV Translation, New Queen Nazareth i.e. Rohs Heat Processed Scalar Enclosure (Protected Workforce Congress, Ecumenical Judification)(Natalie Security Bank Linked)

The Adventist CP i.e. Conceded Pass rating/Oriental Renaissance Benchmark i.e. Nominal rating, Transition Route into Heaven or Express Waiting Gate into Final Heaven.

*Against the Caesar Queen issue Banknote the Hijacked Old Whitehouse (ISIS).
Instead, the Promote of Stellar Head of Fasci UN Chinese issue New Federation Global Class Banknote New Energy Packet, as New Land Property Index. Formed New Chinese Reunion Security Bank, New Whitehouse.
The Famous Red Sea Wall. And Starbucks Currency as omitted remark.

*Total Disruption of ISIS Prime Crime by Chinese Security Activity Technology Stalled Conspiracy of Business Misconduction of Carbonated Licenses and
Church Misconduction Quantum Sky Weapon of Dust Frequency, and Islam Jihad Spiritual World Biblical Villain Misconduction, and Non Tither Church i.e. Philemon, Marriage Misconduction for Erotic Unawareness.

*True Love Bonding, by Mariology Theology i.e. Earth Science Analogy, Physic & Biomedical Constant Protect All kinds of Misconduction Activity, as long as the Quantum Risk Escalating by Universal Official Proof of True Love but not the Least of All Female Kinds the Bottomline Assurance.

Copyright (C) 2023, Ryan Lai Hin Wai, All right reserved.

Y596. Biblical Application: Nativity, Chronicle to Eschatology Calendar Lent Treaty (Broadcast)

Figure 1 (Nazareth the Innocent Victim to Atonement), Christian Persecution, by St. Peterburg i.e. Philemon (Herald)

A. Advent **3G/6G** (8 Cent)(+1min)(Europe Timezone, Geneva)
Military Federation (Orthogonal Classified Benchmark)
low intellect capita (1 Dating, Eschatology i.e. Legend, Orthogonal Affiliation the Meta)
Treasure Era Passover, Post A.D. Lock 10 = 5000 lightyears, Pre A.D. 5000 to A.D. 1
Schism Street Number, Pachelbel Canon in D #9.11 (Parcel, Canonical Biblical Book, C++ Value, Diamond) – Asteroid Rain i.e. Isle Map Greek Rolls, Fire Lake Route
Galatians/Philippian/Colossian/Ephesian/Philemon: Ether, Jobs, John, mmWave (Pentecostal)

B. Renaissance **3.5G/7G** (Dollar)(+6min)(Shanghai Timezone, Greenwich)
Crime Disruption Federal (Pentecostal Ecosystem Mode)
high intellect capita (Etymology i.e. Biography, Biblical Villain the Chronicle Identity)
Treasure Era Lent, A.D. Lock 7 = Alternate Pillar Cycle, Old A.D. 10000 to A.D. 1
Sarah Dust Calendar Blueprint (Projection, Footwell, Cast out), Solar 7th Roman Generations to Olive Earth, Mobile Route
Jude: Nehemiah, Kings, Act, mmGravity (Dating Number)

C. Oriental **1G/5.5G** (3 Cent)(-6min)(New York Timezone, Moscow)
Economic Belt (Aerial Thermal Curve Pi)
low biblical capita (3 Dating, Ecumenical i.e. Credential, Atonement Property with Credential)
Offspring Era Passover, Prior A.D. Lock 4 = Windy, A.D.500 to A.D. 1500
Starbucks Currency Issued Centre (Bytes in Meta, Burner), - Satellite i.e. Coral Island, Sea Route

Titus: Ezra, Chronicle, Revelation, Noel Final Vectorial DNA (Property Lent)

D. Utopia **4G/8G** (Free)(+5min)(London Timezone, Bethlehem)
Credential Centre (Holistic Prism Fibre Histogram)
high biblical capita (4 Dating, Eden Garden i.e. Nativity, Footage of Parallel)
Offspring Era Lent, Pre B.C. Lock 6 = Every year, B.C. 5000 to B.C. 1
Unicorn the Processor (Modular, Thermal Machine), Solver (Patch, Wireless Connector), Coding (Scalar, Shielding Enclosure), Looper (GPU, Eco-Cycle Transducer), Roller (Bios, Wind Miller) – *Jupiter Boosted i.e. Comet Arabic Sequence Dust Collector, Sky Route*
James: Zechariah, Genesis, Luke, Adam Coherent mmDNA (Ergonomics)

E. Utopia 1st **4.5G/9G** (2 Cent)(-5min)(Las Vegas Timezone, Canyon Rock)
Imaginary Olive Nativity (Holy See Meta Story Melodic)
low meta capita (2 Dating, Tree of Fruits i.e. Loyalty, Footwell of Holy Spirit)
Ancestry Time Passover, Old B.C. Lock 1 = 5 days, A.D. 1750 to A.D. 2000
Corinthians Theme Commuter Enclosure in Heat Teleport Chamber & in Light Easter Shell – Mars i.e. Supernova Galaxy, Hell Route
Hebrew: Habakkuk, Thessalonians, Leviticus, Matthew, Abraham Original Chromosome RNA (Currency Deficit)

F. Renaissance Original **5G/10G** (1 Cent)(-1min)(Japan Timezone, Salted River)
Projection Fig Tree Nativity (Holoscopic Meta Number Impressive)
high meta capita (5 Dating, Book of Life i.e. Redemption, Lent of Honey Moon)
Ancestry Time Lent, Old A.D. Lock 9 = Last Day, A.D 1500 to A.D. 2500
Anglican Cathedral the Pentagonal (Anabaptism, Broadcast, Military, Aged Lock, Ruby) – *Moon i.e. Outer Space Latin Series to Black Hole,* Dead End Mileage Route
Corinthians: Malachi, Timothy, Exodus, Mark, Jacob Inaugural Viral mDNA (Correlation Patch Packets)

I. End Time Calendar, a.k.a. Bridegroom Calling (when Mid-Autumn Festival): +1min minus -6min = 5min, Saturday to Sunday
(i.e. Global Class Faith Years),
Japan to Las Vegas = -1 minus -5min->4min (Conjugated Wonderful Days & Faith Days)

II. End Time Occurrence, a.k.a. Heaven Lent (Freehold to Stalled to Renovated) Ticket: 8Cent minus Dollar = -2Cent the Dime Time (Grand, Bytes to Burner)
(i.e. Global Class Player Time the Tournament by Ante), Ante Lent = Original to Original, among many to many->Ether Law of Ashed Skin Marketing Credit equivalent to Currency of Ringgit vs Won->3Cent minus Dollar = -7Cent, Security Exchange Premium.

Y473. Biblical Application: Colour Meta Science Insight (Broadcast)

A. Gold, Diamond: Discrete, 8cent, Silk, Earth (Afternoon), 3.5G
Hue Spot (Scapegoat)(Aerial)(Supremacy) – Politician, Batman (Chancellor)
Malaysia, United States
(Identity Cryptography, Trojan Horse, Utopia Final, **Fire Lake Route**)
Silicon Valley & Diamond Rock, Jerusalem Capital (Moscow Timezone)
– A.D. 1750 to A.D. 2000

B. White, Jade: No, dollar, Crystal, Asteroid (Morning), 3G
Hue Bright (Gentile)(Holoscopic)(Solely) – Mafia, Cat Women (Guardian)
Singapore, Europe Continental
(Body Hosting, Colony, Utopia Alpha, **Mobile Route**)
Modern Desert & Coral Wreckage, Galilee Sea (Greece Timezone)
– A.D. 1500 to A.D. 2500

C. Blue, Sapphire: Wont, 3cent, Calcium, Satellite (Evening), 4.5G
Hue Flash (Sheep)(Orthogonal)(Guru) – Pair, Joker (Caesar)
China
1st Dead, Crime Victim, Renaissance, **Sea Route**
Timber Hill & Gel Jungle, Calvary Hill (Vatican Timezone)
– Pre A.D. 5000 to A.D. 1

D. Pink, Pearl: Raised, free, Fur, Comet (Dusk), 5G
Hue Lantern (Lamb)(Pentecostal)(Payer) – Ace, Guess (oh Carol)
Middle East, Russia
Risen, Chronic Illness, Advent, **Sky Route**
Spiritual High Land & Sand Lake, Bethlehem Town (Geneva Timezone)
– Old A.D. 10000 to A.D. 1000

E. Red, Ruby: Yes, 2cent, Skin, Supernova (Dawn), 4G
Hue Candle (Antichrist)(Holistic)(Attorney) – Lawmaker, Penguin (Age Lock)
Hongkong, South America, Japan, Korea, Australia, New Zealand
2nd Dead, Disaster, **Hell Route**
Milky Mountain & Solar River Zealand, Jordan River (Singapore Timezone)
– A.D. 500 to A.D. 1500

F. Gland, Drug: Can, 1cent, Salt, Solar to Black Hole (Mid Night), 1G
Hue Gland (Goat)(Homogenous)(Heroism) – Revolutionist, Robin (Cupid)
Taiwan, United Kingdom, North Korea, Asia Peninsular
Heritage Footage, Word Prison, Utopia Beta, **All Kind of Castle Route**
Perpetual Grass Land & Smokey Fountain, Nazareth City (London Timezone)
– B.C. 5000 to B.C. 1

Errata 25Dec2022

Y452. Biblical Application: Exodus from Nativity 逃出五指山 (Post)

Three Steps to Heaven

I. Departure: Comet Boost Speed
II. First Contact: Earth Contact Supernova->Star Cube Satellite
III. Loss Contact: Comet Impact Satellite->Planetary Solar System

I. Departure of Comet

The 9 Solar System: 7 Level Heaven. 7 Level Heaven, 1 Fire Lake, 1 Hell.

1th Star, 2nd Star, 3rd Star: Utopia Alpha (Noah Ark), Utopia Beta, Utopia Delta.

4th Star: Hall Mark, Multi-theism Footage (Colourised)
->National Animal 国宝->Ergonomic Standard

5th Star: Kelvin Mark, Monotheism Maturity (Normalisation)
-> National Flower 国花->Cryptography Ranking

6th Star: Data Mark, Trinitarianism Grade (Chronographed)
->National Heritage 国画->Legacy Age

7th Star: Error

8th Star: Venus, 9th Star: Mar, Utopia Lambda, Utopia Sigma.

II. First Contact of Earth to Supernova

1st Batch: Earth (Promised Land), Supernova I (Oriental I)
Noah Ark (Space Ship Temporary Station)->Utopia Alpha

2nd Batch: Earth (Promised Land), Supernova II (Oriental II)
Advent (New Habitat Planet)->Utopia Beta

3rd Batch, 4th Batch: Utopia Delta, Lambda, Sigma, etc.
Continued

III. Loss Contact

Islam ally: Utopia Alpha (Noah Ark) + Utopia Delta Δ, Q, Final (Noah Ark), the Final ->(Time Still & Flying)->Heaven Final (Quantum Heat)

Buddhism ally: Utopia Beta (Eden Garden) + Utopia Gamma Γ, Y, Original (Eden Garden), the Original ->(Animal Telepathy & Space Travel)->Heaven Original (Star Dust)

Hinduism ally: Utopia Omega A (Babel Tower) + Utopia Epsilon E, Z, Express (Babel Tower), the Final ->Heaven Express (Wave)

Islam ally + Buddhism ally + Hinduism ally
(NASA, Automatic, US-AU) vs (CNSA, Manual, CN-RUS) vs (SpaceX, Pilot, UK-JPN)
Christian Persecution vs Semitic Persecution vs Celebrity Persecution
Astronaut, Automatic 车 vs Spaceman, Manual 炮 vs Merchant, Pilot 马
Engineer vs Doctor vs Scientist
6Σ Sigma, Real Number vs 7Λ Lambda, Gravity vs 5Θ Theta, Constant
Kelvin Mark, Add1 vs Data Mark, Sus4 vs Hall Mark, Aug1
->Delta Δ, Final + Gamma Γ, Original + Epsilon E, Express
i.e. Chancellor + Agong + Sultan
Sunni State + Shia Renaissance + Sufism Regime
i.e. Godfather + Pope + Queen
Vatican + Catholic + Episcopal
->Heaven Final/Original + Heaven Original/Final + Heaven Express
(Advent-Quantum) + (Oriental-Star Dust) + (Utopia-Ether)
->Christianity + Charismatic + Six Sigma only the Scapegoat
->Heaven the 7th, Earth the Hell, Fire Lake

Errata 10Dec2022

Y440. Biblical Application: Final Fantasy (Broadcast)

Figure 2 Supernova, the Solar Wave Fusion

Dog 6->Lion 1+Cat 2->Lion/Tiger 1.5

Scissor/Chopstick->Fish->7 star

Dog 6 (Star Cube, Satellite Platform, or Comet the New Earth)
Lion 1 (Supernova Planet>Black Hole)
Cat 2 (Olive Sphere, Earth the Habitat Planet)
Lion liked Tiger 2>1 (Solar Planet)

The 3 Step to Solar Planet, the Sun liked Heaven.

>1. **Stalled Speed and Push Departure: Comet** (Utopia and Promised Land) in which moving at booster speed for star dust collect. (Utopia<>Promised Land)

>2. **The First Contact:** It has the Pentecost Resonance Sniff (Entropy Clock, 0 and 360deg is from Solar) to the Olive Spherical **Earth** (Virgin Olive) before first contact the **Supernova Planet** (Oriental the revelation trial). (Oriental)

>3. **Momentary Loss Contact:** 7 Lightyears required to conjugate the Earth become Solar Dustless Universe, i.e. Heaven. This equivalent to 1 year or 1 year thereafter. (Oriental+Advent->Heaven)

Errata 28Nov2022

Y472. Biblical Application: The Eschatology Suit Correspond the Church Schism (Broadcast)

Chronicle: Individual Meta Science, Cryptography into Chronicle (Season Bill, a.k.a. Remark)(Hormone Bill)
Identity Geography a.k.a. Identity Location/Meta Location (i.e. Port)
A. Cow Boy Suit – 25% Duty, 125% atm – B.C. (Canyon Road Era) - Freedom
Catholic – Democracy, CIA, Hue 73 (Fox) – Silky Skin

B. Wendy Suit – 25% Devotion, 90% atm – Post B.C. (Fairy Tale Era) - Security
Vatican – Oriental Democracy NASA, Hue 37 (Butterfly) – Matted Skin

C. Labour Suit – 20% Duty, 120% atm – A.D. (Buckingham Era) - Renaissance
Fundamentalist – Nationalist, KMT, Hue 66 (Lion) – Creamy Skin

D. Business Suit – 20% Devotion, 75% atm – New A.D. (White House Era) - Mining
Lutheran – Marxism Socialist, WWF, Hue 99 (Mermaid) – Snowly Skin

E. Thither Suit – 10% Duty, 110% atm – Post A.D. (Israel Wall Collapse Era) - Knowledge
Puritan – Republican, NATO, Hue 69 (Dragon) – Metallic Skin

F. African Suit – 10% Devotion, 80% atm – New B.C. (Blue House Era) - Weapon
Charismatic – Fascism Socialist ZION, Hue 96 (Cat) – Glossy Skin

G. Poker Suit – Absolute Duty, 100% atm – End A.D. (Advent Era) - Pilot Heaven
Apostolic – Democrat Socialist, UN, Hue 68 (Rabbit) – Ceramic Skin

H. Mahjong Suit – Duty Free, 1.0 atm – End B.C. (Revelation Era) - Auto Heaven
Episcopal – Monarchy, WHO, Hue 86 (Elephant) – Diamond Skin

Jobs: Homogenous Quantum, Pentecostal from all Jobs (Heritage Bill, a.k.a. Lump)(Carbon + Nicotine Bill)
Nativity Identity a.k.a. Nativity Name/Job Name (i.e. Client)
A. Marketing Clan – Jerusalem (Gold), Goat, IR Candle
B. Sales Clan – Galilee (Jade), Scapegoat, UV Spot
C. Financial Clan – Calvary (Sapphire), Gentile, UV Bright
D. Accounting Clan – Bethlehem (Pearl), Sheep, ESD Flash
E. Technical Clan – Jordan (Ruby), Lamb, EMF Lantern
F. Personnel Clan – Nazareth (Drug), Antichrist, EMF Gland

Exodus: Holistic Pilgrim Footage, Lent Grounded on Exodus (Intellectual Bill, a.k.a. Fee)(Toxic Bill)
Virginia Nativity a.k.a. Virginia God/Pilgrim God (i.e. Host)

A. Jurassic Park Timeline – Very High Lent (Australia), Bethlehem (Geneva +5min)

B. Mission Impossible Timeline – Lent free (Israel), Jordan (Singapore -5min)

C. Hollywood Timeline – Small Lent (United States), Jerusalem (Moscow +1min)

D. Star War Timeline – High Lent (Hongkong), Nazareth (London -1 min)

*Highlights: The Climate Threat could change a City into Black Hole Darkness Era in which vulnerable for War Crime.

Y473. Biblical Application: Colour Meta Science Insight (Broadcast)

A. Gold, Diamond: Discrete, 8cent, Silk, Earth (Afternoon), 3.5G
Hue Spot (Scapegoat)(Aerial)(Supremacy) – Politician, Batman (Chancellor)
Malaysia, United States
(Identity Cryptography, Trojan Horse, Utopia Final, **Fire Lake Route**)
Silicon Valley & Diamond Rock, Jerusalem Capital (Moscow Timezone)
– A.D. 1750 to A.D. 2000

B. White, Jade: No, dollar, Crystal, Asteroid (Morning), 3G
Hue Bright (Gentile)(Holoscopic)(Solely) – Mafia, Cat Women (Guardian)
Singapore, Europe Continental
(Body Hosting, Colony, Utopia Alpha, **Mobile Route**)
Modern Desert & Coral Wreckage, Galilee Sea (Greece Timezone)
– A.D. 1500 to A.D. 2500

C. Blue, Sapphire: Wont, 3cent, Calcium, Satellite (Evening), 4.5G
Hue Flash (Sheep)(Orthogonal)(Guru) – Pair, Joker (Caesar)
China
1st Dead, Crime Victim, Renaissance, **Sea Route**
Timber Hill & Gel Jungle, Calvary Hill (Vatican Timezone)
– Pre A.D. 5000 to A.D. 1

D. Pink, Pearl: Raised, free, Fur, Comet (Dusk), 5G
Hue Lantern (Lamb)(Pentecostal)(Payer) – Ace, Guess (oh Carol)
Middle East, Russia
Risen, Chronic Illness, Advent, **Sky Route**
Spiritual High Land & Sand Lake, Bethlehem Town (Geneva Timezone)
– Old A.D. 10000 to A.D. 1000

E. Red, Ruby: Yes, 2cent, Skin, Supernova (Dawn), 4G
Hue Candle (Antichrist)(Holistic)(Attorney) – Lawmaker, Penguin (Age Lock)
Hongkong, South America, Japan, Korea, Australia, New Zealand
2nd Dead, Disaster, **Hell Route**
Milky Mountain & Solar River Zealand, Jordan River (Singapore Timezone)
– A.D. 500 to A.D. 1500

F. Gland, Drug: Can, 1cent, Salt, Solar to Black Hole (Mid Night), 1G
Hue Gland (Goat)(Homogenous)(Heroism) – Revolutionist, Robin (Cupid)
Taiwan, United Kingdom, North Korea, Asia Peninsular
Heritage Footage, Word Prison, Utopia Beta, **All Kind of Castle Route**
Perpetual Grass Land & Smokey Fountain, Nazareth City (London Timezone)
– B.C. 5000 to B.C. 1

玫瑰经 Marriage Tither and Duty for Total Sovereign of God becoming class A1 zero terrorism lift up.

"Lord of Lord, have Mercy upon us, have mercy upon us. Freedom is too much" N times

Y359. Puritan Music Part 1: Understanding Of Coding (Post)

A. Chord Progression: Biblical
B. Scale: Soul
C. Lyrics: Holy Spirit
D. Melody: Quantum
E. Rhythm: Pentecost
F. Tempo: Spiritual Body

Tempo: It is by Heart Beat 60 beat per minute (i.e. The most Smallest discrepancy from those Breath Compensation).
60 b.p.m. (50% percentile), Church Pace

106 b.p.m (75% percentile), Folks Pace

14 b.p.m (25% percentile), Children Pace

Rhythm: Hence, the Coding is $60/133.33=9/40$. The 1/8 beats is the 1st Ranking at 10% compensation rate. 2nd Ranking is 1/16 beats at 12.5% compensation rate. And walts the 1/3 beats at 22.5% compensation rate, 1/6 beats at 22.5% compensation, the maximum compensation can reach is about 25%.
Illustration as,

1/8 Rock and Sentimental (Church Pace)

1/16 Rock' & Roll and Tango (Children Pace)

1/3 Slow Rock and Walts (Folks Pace)

Y363. Puritan Music Part 1b: Lyrics & Melody Coding (Post)

Lyrics the Quantised also the verse: It is the Linearity algorithm by the differ on the maturity of the Music Piece, it is a cause and effect mode.

Hence, the Coding of **Lyrics** has 4 Phase in a verse. It is begin with **Pizz**, and then **Aftertouch**, follow by **Attack**, last phase **Bow**.

And the Quantised Code is e.g. 1/8, 2/8, etcs. It is perfected describe by ASCII notification of Pizz, Aftertouch Attack and Bow, e.g. ZZZ, SSS, CCC, WWW. and "+" and "++", or -, and "–", as the subscript.
It has to highlight that the verse is predicting played by specific music scale mode as well as decorated by the harmony principle e.g. music harmony interval.
Melody the pitch also the loop: It is also the Scheme of the music, a loop i.e. sequence of verse by intro, chorus and ending.

It has to highlighted that the melody is predicting played by specific chord progression.
The Coding thereby, 7+2, Hex Graphical i.e. Chromatic Colour Hue, full stop.
The Chord progression is corresponded to the melody played, vice versa. The Music Scale Theorem Notation not belong this category, but it is addressed in latter paragraph.

Y360. Puritan Music Part 2: Music Genre Recognition (Post)

Brother: a. Music Pitch Law
Son: b. Music Scale Theorem
Sister: c. Music Tone Technique
Mother: d. Music Harmony Principle
Father: e. Music Scheme Theory

There are in combination progressive filtered on and escalating to better music genre until present and foresee future, since the Buckingham era when the established piano music invented.

This is called Music Evolution, but better understand it in Music Retro and Music Reformation, due to it is up down fluctuated along with Economy progression at large scale.

To name a few **Music Retro Era**,

i. Blues (Commercial)<>Soul (Music Retro Era)(Israel the Heaven Era form up, minimum to Palestine)

ii. Choral (Devout)<>Drum

iii. Classical (Stable)<>Lullaby (Music Retro Era)(Germany Industrial Revolution)

iv. Symphony (Steady)<>Tango

v. Hymn (Meta)<>Classic (Music Retro Era)(Church Reformation)

vi. Folks (Nature)<>Ethnic

vii. Jazz (Orbit)<>Hill

viii. Rock (Worship)<>Metal (Satanic)

ix. Baroque (Self Healing)<>Psycho (Music Retro Era)(Western Culture Renaissance)

x. New Age (Baby Boom)<>Sentimental

This could repeated and improvised but these are the boundary of Music Genre.

Copyright (C) 2022, Ryan Lai Hin Wai, All right reserved.

Y364. Puritan Music Part 2a: Music Scale Theorem & Music Pitch Law (Post)

Music Scale Theorem
a. Suspended Scale **7+2, G, D, the 42th**, Piano, Hymn (Booming)(Dove) – **Heaven**
b. Added Scale **7+4, B, F, the 84th**, Keyboard, Jazz – **Hell**
c. Major Scale **7+0, C, the 105th**, Cello, Classical (Crisis)(Dove)
d. Minor Scale **7-2, B, the 6th**, Violin, Ethnicity
e. Augmented Scale **7+3, D, B, 63th,** Brass, Blues (Recession)(Eagle) – **Paradise**
f. Diminished Scale **7-3, D, 9th**, Flute, Oldies – **Poverty**
g. Dominant Scale **7+1, C G, the 21th**, Acoustic Guitar, Rock
h. Sub-Dominant Scale **7-1, F, the 3rd**, Classical Guitar, Folks (Downturn)(Eagle)

The Insight: The Eagle and Dove of Music a.k.a. Circle of Fifth
Do Re Mi Fa So La Ti Do

Do vs So vs Re vs Ti vs Fa

C, G, D, B, F

The Theorem: Meta Law Discrepancy
*This is about the Order sequence of **Meta Law Discrepancy** in which the Spiritual Ranking defined as Spiritual Maturity. Its a 360 deg, and make up the 8 Segment corresponded to the Scaled Volume the Music Network which is also the World Wide Network. It can be corresponded to **Chord Progression**, in which the well known Circle of Fifth was defined.

The 7+2 is the Meta Law Standard as Predefined, for it is the Cryptography of Quantum Dynamics, or Simply the Organic Maturity, hence the Meta Law can only capture to either Majority Man or Majority Female, in which called Eagle and Dove, connected the Heaven and Earth.

The Doctrine of Heaven and Earth, differ in Dimensioning of God. The Hymn vs Blue is like Heaven Music and Paradise Music.

Clarification required on Evil or Holiness Music. From Meta Law Discrepancy it couldn't tell the Evil or Holiness but Sovereign of God.

Music Pitch Law
The Frequency of Musical Tone is called Pitch. And to archive the Quantum Escalating Knots, it had to be 7 Full Pitch, and 5 Semi Pitch, make up total 12 Musical Note.

The Frequency of those 7 Full Pitch is Linearity start at the 440 HZ for referendum of Resonance Fork, as the Datum Note Frequency. It has depend on discrepancy on the Atmosphere condition, yielding different Bandwidth Quality of Sound Texture. This is directly corresponding to the Music Scale. The Harmony Principle should follow upon these.

The Linearity maintain, as well as the Linearity rate maintain, for the same Music Scale, Full Stop.

Music Harmony Principle
The Music Harmony is not affected by Physical Atmosphere Condition but depend on the Music Scale, in which the category of Music Instrument is defined.

Music Harmony has to be designed to comply to each Music Instrument in brief, hence it has to be tolerance on the discrepancy of Music Pitch the Sound Texture.

For 12 Music Note, the Music Harmony is defined as where the Semitone filled in. For Example Piano, and String Music Instrument, in which 2 type of Linearity Layout the Music Scale to be corresponded And under the String Music Instrument. there are dozens of Linearity Layout to be configurated.

And Music Harmony Standard is defined as Music Interval, instead of Pitch distance.

Illustration:
Do Re Mi Fa So La Ti Do

Pitch distance has 6 equal quantised.

But Music Interval has 7+5 at Maximum to 7-3 at Minimum.

The Music Interval corresponded to Music Scale, and Music Linearity Layout, as simple as that.

Music Tone Technique
To Change the Music Tone i.e. Sound Texture is to Change the Linearity Line to be Curvature. Hence, the Resonance energy would be at loss, but to archiving the distorted Sound Texture for Performing needs.

Y361. Puritan Music Part 3: Symphony Hierarchy (Post)

4 Music Ministry: Bass, Drum, Brass, String

10 of Music Graded Track: Solo, Accompany, Decoration make up 3 Bandwidth Standard.

Conductor the Sequencer: The Bottom Graded is the Most Standard Performing, and the Upper Graded is the Conductor who play the Full Free Styled on Music Tempo, and Music Scheme.

Lead the Lyrics Track: Entire Playback is focus on the Lyrics Description, perform by the Lead Track. Usually the Most Busy One, but depend on the Solo portion, Accompany portion and Decoration portion ratio.

Y389. Social Engineering VI: Humanity Heritage is the keyhold of Heaven (Forum)

There arent enough. There is rootcause we had determined. They are not belong to us. One word is not enough. This is called the downfall of Light House.

One man dreams. Its the victory of us. People are running forward now. Those are good one. Make a straight one. Continues important. It is proportional. Let backup.

So what is license meant? It mean original. Wrong Montage could make Genocide and End an Community.

Please don't living in Abstract. This is Devil. Freed yourself, you find back yourself. Terrorism jealous against our Career. False Teaching jealous against our Community. Virus Toxic jealous against our Erotic.

Those jealous, against Jesus, those no jealous, aliked Jesus.

To cure Jealous is to start from your Job or Business. Money can't help. This is Nationalism and Capitalism. What everybody lack is the Montage.

This required Travelling and Finding Ancestry. This is the Government doesnt want to let you know.
Some belief the Past Life, or Biblical Character. This is about the All the Time Ranking of Community.
Its Flip down escalating.

Man dominated versus Women dominated. The Diaspora versus Indigenous. And this is both attraction, by one positive and negative.

Hence, it could form up alot of communities, ranked by the diaspora. It is International. The indigenous, could form up a strong community by Scale. Not so easy. Quota versus Scale

But those Ethnic has strong montage has this benefit. Its about Genealogy the Post Natal instead, not Genetic.

Some country hiding their past crime, for getting better Montage. Its fictional. You attract the Folks only.

Spanish are particular about this.

To build up a community is a keyhold on Religion Protest. Christianity Reformation is International 4 axis oriented, the Economy Milestone only, but Christianity Evolution is Universal 5 axis, the Heritage milestone could made by this.

Hence the World War is Pre-Advent A.D, and Cold War is Post-Advent A.D. The Delay of 30 years is Cold War.

It is a journey from World War to Cold War. The timing is 111 year the small loop of geography pioneer, and also the big loop of heaven pioneer the 1000 years.

There was High Bandwidth Box Office. It can be replicating many and many, by making even smaller loop. The Quality of Jew Community make distinguish of it.

The Jew community is the Lever, the Bottleneck. It is contrasting with Jude Community. This is the Datum of referendum of any other communities which can even higher.

Not Market share and Pie. The Qualitative Value. The Dollar sign. What we compete is not the community, its about the Heritage.

Let all community develop their economic myth. We will fight it with 4 kind of Heritage Symbol. Pound Dollar Sterling and Yuan.

That is the meaning of Cold War. Who rules the Heaven. Islam, Buddhism, Christian and Christmas.

The Famous 4 heritage. If only the Pound and Sterling has all said. This decides Marriage Protection Act. The Mariology.

Spanish "Romance de Amour", French "Ballad of Adeline". In other Asia Culture is Closed Borders Strategy. e.g. The North Korea.

They want Economy Myth but Not the Currency. To join Islam and Christianity we get Buckingham.
Buddhism and Christianity also Buckingham, the Pound vs Sterling.

The Bulks or Yuan is general meaning. The Dollar the alternative to Bulks. Hence, there is no other Alternative for Israel Diplomacy with Palestine.

The Victory determine who rules the Heaven, the Pound or Dollar.

This yield 2 kind of heaven, the Material dominated or Spiritual dominated. The Tailor made or Spiritual harmony.

Moon icon is Dollar, the Star is Pound, and Cross is Sterling. Meta, Social and Montage. Utopia, Promised Land and Oriental.

The coverage is important. Its about the size of Pacific rim. The Radius of two Economy myth premises. Make the Promised Land and Oriental, hence deduce the Next.

But its a referendum only, take the radius as closure. Its more likely Dollar. Its just tailor made, and we are all the tailor.

Talk about technology, the Pound meta is Replica Engineering the Macintosh. the Sterling meta is Holistic Engineering the Ferrari. And Dollar meta is Automation Engineering the Printer.

Macintosh is about Colour Hue, Ferrari is about Texture, and HP is about Embodiment. There 3 brand maturity age is 8 x 10 years.

The Reverse Engineering determine the Maturity Strength.
Terrorism is Equal to World War. Winner is not just theory.

For who follow the Edge, conquer the Death, and Heaven. From Death to Heaven is a journey of high bandwidth Road, Canyon road, Silk road.

When you walk in, you will walk out. Just follow. Temptation can change the course. You will be challenge with your strength. Not your least.

Natalism vs Racialism. Natalism is no question. But Racialism was used as Semiticism. This is misinformation. Impossible, semitic ethnic has the strongest social bonding.

So if someone claim Semitic is Racist this is the Germanic. Natalism is Horoscope oriented. Same as Charismatic, the Germans play around Evil Power. Alienic.

Protestant church is Episcopal, Church Reformed. Charismatic Church is Vatican, Church Evolution.
The Enemy of Episcopal has Two.

The Martyr and Christian Persecution. The Imperialism Catholic advocate Christian Persecution.
And the Vatican Serve Public ministry to make sustainable church.

Price is Martyr. Anti Semitic is Anti Natalism. Racist is against Islam. Islam make distanced from Public Ministry. Hence, Germanic vs British

To gain 3 axis of Meta, we required diminished the Bulks. No loose method but tight method. Its not testing but series of trial.

No note taking, but Safety precaution. This is the diamond, no testing or experimental required.

The International Community Natalism versus Nation Wide Community Racist. The Meta Science is perfectionism, no tolerance. Dangerous.

Ban Abstract Social Engineering. That is poverty. Natalism is not for Rich either. But Country Wealth.

So the 1 datum plane fixed, the 4 datum plane are random, it would self oriented. This is diamond making.

Dark Energy is Free Energy a.k.a. Potential energy at no temperature change. This is the Light Bulb tungsten and Fluorescent light. For magic has thief, technology no thief. Sow and Reap.

It is abundant to give, but cant received. Begin with ancient Chinese know this, until today same. The Holy Spirit by Grace.

You gain what you want free. Wealth is not about Hardwork, its about Choosing the right platform.
Example, more people more help.

Its Space Craft. It is more inclined toward Veterinary the Surgery Medicine. No end. Until we make the Meta to Moses Law the Dollar, that is the Final Journey.

The Holistic Engineering Calls. Not Blockchain but Supply Chain. This how Rocket can make. Not All Rocket same.

Modular, Screw-less, Dashed, Lubricated to name the fours. Modular Dollar, Screw-less Pound, Dashed Sterling, Lubricated Yuan.

All other Business correspond from these Big Four. Correspond to JDM Holistic Engineering, OBM Replica Engineering, OEM Theoretical Engineering, ODM Reverse Engineering. This is too popular. What I highlighted is we need moving forward from Technology to Humanity.

In other words, the New Government. Diminished Terrorism for Politic benefit. We need money talk and Humour.

This is in Between Natalism and Racist, inclined toward Democracy. Without Datum fixed on Democracy, we cant make 6 axis Diamond, Humanity Heritage.

This is to trigger all Heritage growth. That the end, choose right platform you will no terrorism.
Heaven automatic form up, when people join in.

The Famous Three People Management. The making of Logistic mechanism of commuting people to Wealthy place.

The Nation Wide only. Be careful of the Datum. It must be upright. For Whatever, it will run and to the finished. Cannot Pilot Run.

When Heritage become Maturity, it would time lock, the story begin from thence. It is not now, but anytime.

No magic here, its eye feast. Not blink of eye, but progressive very slowly. Its 111 years required. For any Economic Body reach Maturity.

For those high Performer. Who make the bottom neck. The Logistic Concept, loading of one is free.
This is skeptic, the pioneer of discovery is Messenger. Concurrent is contradict.

So, make friend in telephone, make enemy in internet, make love in bed. Placebo effect. The perpetual is the bonding with Jew.

For Breaking the Social Bond, is breaking the Law. That is upmost in Heaven. Not Mixed. or Harmony.
I dont know how to say.

You way is my way, my way is not your way. Hence 5 axis diamond grouping is the best methodology.
Expandable into 1 layer. The famous 10 conjugate.

Let make the predictable heaven to total heaven. All is begin with a journey, and we are half way done.
Too many Heritage we accumulated. We cannot afford Start over.

New thinking come out. New Future. Linear thinking cannt. Must become Decisive. For Soccer Ball is predictable Ball. Its link up past and future. Called Moles effect.

In brief everything can count. But you cannot count Jesus. Uncountable, and become to Atonement.
He will resurrection you too.

This is not just ritual, but the sign of trust. Reflected on Church and Holy Spirit and Election. Hence, there are 12 symbol of Cross.

You cannot group it into one. Its real number. This number is 5 axis right? Ortho view break it. The Real number value tell the Scaled of Montage.

The God wills. Its you make the God wills, not God wills make you. Its plenty of God wills, the job. And, you will have abundancy and eternal life.

All road lead to Heaven, but not all road fit you. Choose the one you can get. Winner can be only one.
Love is required in Heaven.

Its not right to abolished Law, its the Einstein Law. This Law is the Moses Law. If you don't understand Law, you don't understand Love. Love is belong to Law.

Its free energy. All is free.

Its at the expense of the yeast of atonement. This is Church business Operating manual. Not by Forcing, but Supporting the least one.

The very least, contribution. Those have new love definition, has New God. I meant the New Direction.
This could make people fall down. We cannt change God.

This is very single most important rule. This is about your Soul and Body. Its similar to God eyes. Hence, its relativity, no right or wrong.

But Quality high or low. This make the pillar of justice or evil. Sow and Reap. The time dilation of body response is the Justice Maturity.

This is can bring you to accident. It is journey of begin to finish, a sequencer journey. This can be used on Cloud Computing. The Next Home Car.

Most important is used on Watch Product. Its Satellite.

When the time progressive, we are more prompted to Legitimate.

Pound, Episcopal i.e. Christianity Reformation, (Natalism)(Semitic Supremacy), Honda, **Trade Secret** i.e. Trademark, Replica Engineering – Engine

Dollar, Islam, Catholic, Islam+Episcopal (Secularistic), IBM, Market Survey i.e. **Service Mark**, Holistic Engineering – Suspension

Sterling, Vatican i.e. Christianity Evolution, (Racialism)(White Supremacy), Ferrari, Economic Review i.e. **Copyright**, Linear Engineering – Chassis

Yuan, Buddhism, Charismatic, Buddhism+Charismatic, (Artistic) Samsung, Whitepaper i.e. **Patent**, Theoretical Engineering – Drivetrain

Y454. Social Engineering X: World Threats & Rootcause (Forum)

I. Diaspora: Those Non Clan
Spiritual Body/Soul->Lamb/Gentile

Genocide for Nazi Heritage (Semitic Persecution)
Utopia of Harps Theory
B1. Trojan Horse: Make Erotic Defect (False Accuser)
C2. Heritage Frauding: Moron Injection & Quarantine
C1. Chronic Illness Fraud: Virus to Pandemic
B2. Economic Conspiracy: New World Order & False Teaching

II. Orthodox: Those Non Schism
Holy Spirit/Evil Spirit->Sheep/Antichrist

Terrorism for Cult Heresy (Christian Persecution)
Charismatic Wave of African Supremacy
E2. Word Prison: Make Language Defect (Word Masking)
A1. Tragedy: Electric & Torturing
F1. Famine Conspiracy: Jobless to Jobless Rate
A2. Religion Conspiracy: Terrorism for Migration & Technology Scamming

III. Inhouse: Those Non Shoe
Pentecost/Ghost->Goat/Scapegoat

Disaster for Mafia Heaven Critics (Celebrity Persecution)
Social Engineering Genocide of One Way Ticket
D1. Colony: Make Literacy Defect (Identity Thief)
F2. Mind Poisoning & Toxic: False Drug & Food & Beverage Drug
E1. God Misconduction Threat: Accident to Disaster
D2. Technology Conspiracy: Medicine Genocide & Mind Poison

*Rootcause: Prime Chain of Heresy (e.g. Utopia or Charismatic Wave, or Social Engineering Genocide) + 6 Biblical Villain

Y406. Social Engineering VIII: What Movie Box Office Tells? (Forum)

Bandwidth 3 Closure.

A. Media Technology

B. Scene Working Teams

C. Casting Role playing

Hence, Bandwidth translated to Box Office, and indicating the Computer Literacy Level of Audience.
And the Computer Literacy is the Social Ranking.
High Box Office is undoubtably a trend of Economic Crisis.

Copyright (C) 2022, Ryan Lai Hin Wai, All right reserved.

Y442. Social Engineering VIV: Copycat Workforce Management (Forum)

A. Marketing
Drama & Story Scripting – Anti False Teaching (Information Distrust Endervour)

B. Sales
Sound & Action Producer – Anti Tragedy (Hall Mark a.k.a. Sound & Colour Graded), Anti Disaster (Kelvin Mark a.k.a. Quantum Number), Anti Meditation (Artwork Quality Mark a.k.a. Discrete & Truncate Footage)

C. Financial
Box Office & Fund Affiliation – Anti Genocide (Data Protection Mark)

D. Accounting
Director & Editor – Anti Poisoning (Censorship & Mask Timer)

E. Technical
Dialogue & Subtitle – Anti Technology Scamming (Advertisement Fund)

F. Personnel
Casting & Anticipator – Anti Heritage Frauding (Credential Mark the Hatred Privacy Recognition)

Y491. Social Engineering XII: The Key Christian The Stakeholder & Key Christian Town The Safety Footage (Forum)

A. Pentagon (Mafia Underground): **HAWAII** (ZION)(KMT)
False Royalism, War & Heritage, Jack
Intelligence: Man of Sins, Sea King
(Misconduction War & Heritage)
Thermal Network 3G, Telescope Coherent Wave, Cable Modem, Fax, Parametric Data)
– Manual Made Virus #4 by Parametric Solver the High Experiment Dependency Algorithm
Pilgrim Footage Alert

Imperial Palace Japan (Nazi Regime): GER (WHO)

B. Istana Palace (Mafia Organised): SG (NATO)(Jerusalem)
The Axis: Devil, White Dragon Long
(Misconduction Business & Government), World Bank the Mining Funding Military Regime
Management Fee (Personnel)
False Doctrinal, Business & Government, King, Levi & Jew, Democracy Tax Collector (Intellectual)
(Epsilon Analog Hue Geothermal Network 1G, Nanotechnology, Dark Magic Ergonomic Overwrite, Quantum Bug Code, Private Calendar)
– Autopilot Control, Tsunami by Universe's Ulra-Nano Wave #3
Criminal Alert

Blue House (Fasci Recruit Campaign): JPN (FBI)

C. White House (Qing Syndicate Scapegoat *Hijack): US (UN)(NASA)
False Democracy, Engineering & Education, Pope
False Prophet, **Ransom Tendency:**
The Antichrist & Anti Chinese, Fox/Rabbit/Owl/Cat
(Misconduction Engineering & Education)
(Antenna Network 5G, The Pentecostal Wave, Seismic Alert in Hours, Months, Decade)
– #2 DNA Genocide by Remote Controlled Nuclear
Prophecy Calendar Alert

Iskandar Palace (Fasci Think Tank): MY (CIA)

D. Buckingham Palace (Nazi Economy Body): UK (WWF)
False Ministry, Medicine & Banking, Queen
Dangerous to Heroic: False Christ, White Dragon Short
(Misconduction Medicine & Banking)
(Brain Receiver, Telecom Electrical Network 3.5G, Wire Cable)

– the Erotic Defect #1 when Colour Hue Scale Up, Triggered the Conditional non Specific Terrorism
Christian Organisation Alert

Grand Palace Thailand (Qing Syndicate Funding): THAI (World Bank)(Vatican)

Y493. Social Engineering XIII: Carrier & Carrier Loading (Forum)

A. Land the Mileage: Life Span & Expendency
Clan Milestone divided by Body Ageing
Youth Rabbit: Luxury Mileage (Couples) – Prophet (Parents)
Old Horse: Rusted Mileage (Maverick) – Revolutionist (Fans)
Child Dragon: Commuting Mileage (Hollywood) – Guardian (Cupid)
Fat Monkey: Dead End Mileage (Athlete) – Idol (Scholar)

B. Sky Load the Margin: Air Leaked & Resort Planet
Ether Percentile Time Lapsed
1cent: River to/from Fountain
Dollar: Sea to/from Lake
Valley, Coral Sea, **Alternate Core**: 8cent (Evil Sprit)
Coral Island, Basin, **Extra Core**: Dollar (Antichrist)
Hill, Isles, **Extra Terrestrial**: 3cent (False Holy Spirit)
Lake, Deep Sea, **Extra Time**: free (Young Holy Spirit)
River, Triangle, **Extra Skyline**: 2cent (Ghost)
Fountain, Strait, **Extra Dimensions**: 1cent (Gentile)

C. Sea Harbour the Time Lapsed: Identity & Calligraphy Ranked
Ether Percentage Per Capita Individual Divided by Ether Percentile Gross
Lapsed, Nation/International/Universal

Doctor: Vet vs Mental
Manager: Crew the Coder vs Captain the Translator
Astronaut: Lab vs Metro
Christian Sheep, Capita Goat: **Intellect (Counter)**
Christian Goat, Capita Sheep: **Natalie (Roulette)**
Christian Lamb, Capita Gentile: **Star (Baroque)**
Christian Gentile, Capita Lamb: **Rock (Scout)**

Y496. Social Engineering XIII: Social Weapon the Capital Redemption Islam (Forum)

*West Asia the Peninsular ally West Asia the Offshore
Promised Land Final Trial Number ally Utopia Land Original Generations
Islam Noel ally Utopia the #24
Diamond Suit the vs Omega Suit the Contemporary

A. **Christian Ministry**: Freed Supremacy 自由至上主义
Brute Force Vulnerable (Nazi Fasci), due Public Critics
Technology, Engineering
James, St. Paul vs Cruel Doer (False Prophet)
Military Technology, Eschatology Calendar, Apostolic
Shia Islam ally Islam Prayer
Gendik i.e. **Agong** equi. the Royal Minister vs Lambda #24
Marxism Socialist, **Non Islam King** vs Fasci Socialist, **Royal Doctor**
Batik, Sarong for _Non Islam_, Illegal Clergy (Licensed Free)
Toxic Bill, for Quarantine Immunity, a Blood Cell Price

B. **God Ministry:** Marriage Supremacy 婚姻至上主义
Frauding Vulnerable (Mafia Fasci), due Tither Critics
Economics, Medicine
Joshua, St. Joseph vs Lunatic Head (Devil)
Economic Treasure, Theology Research, Catholic, Christian Preaching
Sunni Islam ally Islam Renaissance
Keris i.e. **Prophet** equiv. the Royal Engineer vs RQ
Federal Banking, **Non Cult Queen** vs Capita Regime, **Colonel**
Penlagan, Nyonya for _Non Cult_, Illegal Labour (Loyal Free)
Poison Bill, for Lawsuit Immunity, a Textile Brick Price

C. **Public Ministry:** White Supremacy 白人优先主义
Scamming Vulnerable (Organised Fasci), due Private Critics
Business, Music
Santa Claus, St. Peter vs Dirty Thinker (False Christ)
Religion Unity, Christian Ecumenical, Discipleship, Christian Reformation
Sufism Islam ally Islam States
Pending i.e. **Final Sultan** the Royal Lawyer vs RY
Constitutional Monarchy, **Non Tither Jack** vs Democrat Socialist,
President
Datuk, Datin for _Non Tither_, Illegal Business (Duty Free)
Hormone Bill, for Revenge Immunity, a First Night Price

Y527. Social Engineering XV: The Chinese Democracy Framework (Forum)

A. Reflection/Imaginary: Rib of Man, the Hormone Age Lock
Heaven: Final Utopia Carrier for Love Alone
Original Heaven:
Kingkong the Spy vs Pope the Pastor ally Rabbi/Chang'er (Final Touch, True Love)
Graded Heaven:
Desperado the Saint vs Chancellor the Apostle ally Mickey/Diamond Queen (Retouch, Artistic)
Sea Gate: Hosting, the Portable Archive, Station
Natalie: Capped, Capitalism, Goat, Dust
Security: House or Mileages
Chinese Reunion Fellowship (Capital, Business Suit none Alternate Core Refugee i.e. Trojan Horse)
The Intellectual Bank, <u>Security Premier</u>

B. Decryption/Encryption: Rib of Man, the Carbon Judi Lock
Utopia: Promised Land Milestone for Final Marriage
Renaissance:
Guru the Prestige vs Royal Doctor the Founder ally Scholar/Club (Decryption, Pluto)
Advent:
Batman the Discreet vs Banker the Proprietary ally Club/Bunny (After Touch, Agape)
Land Rover: Fire Wall, the Telecommunication Capsule, Outpost
Commuting: Car or Cards
Tither: Ashed, Materialism, Lamb, Matter
Christian Organisation (Zone per Capita, Christian Clan none Virginia Diaspora i.e. Word Prison)
The Natalie Congress, <u>Judi Initiative</u>

C. Schematic/Sketch: Rib of Man, the Nicotine Spiritual Lock
Eden Garden: Lock Eden Garden for Last Resort
Oriental the Lock Eden Garden:
Mafia the Freelance vs Colonel the Poet ally Bann List/Royal
Utopia the Extra Eden Garden:
Maverick the Public Service vs President the Poet ally Royal/*Monalisa*?
Sky App: Client, the Universal Satellite, Remote
Backup: Wall or Wars
Intellect: Inked, Socialism, Sheep, Medium
Democracy Framework (Gross Capita, Cells Schism none Organised Whitelist i.e. Colony)
The Neighbourhood Consultancy, <u>Privilege Ministry</u>

Y528. Social Engineering XVI: The Premium Security Trade Mistake due Conjugating Calendar Montage to Legacy, e.g. Atonement to Redemption of Non-Carry Tither (Forum)

i. Democrat Socialist, Royal, the Totalitarianism
– 资本经济特区
Spectra to Maverick

ii. The Fasci Socialist, Royal Traitor, Apostles, the Dictatorship
– 直接管辖经济特区
Organised to Blacklist

iii. Marxism Socialist, Regime Repel, Pastor
–日不落经济特区
Organised to Whitelist

iv. Nationalist, Congressional Constitution
– 卫星租界物流集合港口 B Class 高科技自动化军事医药 - 经济承载规格技术
Equality to Judification

v. Oriental Democracy, Imperial Constitution
– 电缆租界临床实验室 C Class 泛科技系统化工业医药 - 宇宙统筹规格技术
Spectra to Bankruptcy

vi. Republican, Liberal Constitution
– 无线电租界商业区 F Class 虚拟科技医药等工业量子化 -计算机导航规格技术
Mafia Minor to Lawsuit

vii. Monarchy Democracy, Holy See Constitution
– 天线租界轻工业园 A Class 草根科技医等工业模组化 -电脑泛生规格技术
Judification to Glorification

viii. Monarchy Democrat, Regime
–自治经济特区
Mafia Major to Penalty

The Security Trade Off Mistake: 1) Nun Marriage & 2) *Non Tither Carrier*
三八线冲锋准则，无花果准则，末世准则，别当真

Monarchy Democracy Vatican and Buckingham 99th *Lost and Found Sheep, a number to Unlimited Baby Booms.* The Dragons the Intellects the Primary Workforce for all Industrial to Economy Carrier.

Nationalist or Oriental Democracy the 101 Lock Lion Girl

Y552. Social Engineering XVII: Luohan & Whitelist (Forum)

World War
Disruption of Fasci Socialist Genocide Organised.
18 Luohan the Think Tank Pilgrim Footage.

Cold War
Disruption of Nazi Scapegoat Climate Change Conspiracy
Democrat Military Regime and Royalism Congress Whitelist.

Y467. Journey To Bethlehem, The Christmas Town (Forum)

Awaken Call, 1st. Freedom Marriage. 2nd. Semitic Exodus.

The King Made Ethnic better than Man Made Ethnic.

Make your own Legislation.

Murder king. I mean all kings.

My dick harder than you. Standing on the solid rock. Error coding cant make colour.

I lose my patience. But this is the fact we need to accept. We are under attack. If you follow me, you will keep follow. If you are finding troubles, its your right.

I have my right and record to stand aside you all. But I would never had did that. Back to the topic, I am finding solid reason to rule out the mythical that we burden.

This is apparently a star war gig.

Or just a Nut house issue. Noises speech I don't mine, but straight to the south. This a dilemma to make, but most concerns.

The Law of Democracy still around the Persecution of Mental. This a world wide and nationwide against Christmas and Churches.

Hence from this small clinched, the answer may solved. And reason of this is not political protest nor Sudden War.

Its to increase the Signature of Righteous. We are no human right to Against the Crime Syndicate, by all proper means.

Hence, following is head to the south.

Our Cross Atonement, Corner Stone and Redemption is Strengthen by Allergy. Without Allergy we and all Church have nothing.

Ir-regardless number of trials, but all are welcome. The only reason stopping the allergy is same king gather.

So back to the Medicine Issue. Church has loss their Duty. This is Crime Syndicate Funding, not Charity Funding. Mafia is down and more down.

When Church backed by Nazi. This is a Cult.

Show me your atonement.

You are running a dead end church. And Without Church without Medicine. This is the Top down Hierarchy.

If you anti Nationalist Speech, then I cant talk other things to you. You are not the group of people. Most. All dead.

This is not hatred, but Peeper. You will have to set your own time.

My Clear list has no anti Human.

Doing the sneak, and you find your new place again. I cant worship you.

Sons of Israel, you are freed. No more tata.

Seems I banned. Too much bulletin.

This is not my Host.

You may make your own law, there more and more law you can applied. If you like. But this is no cure.

The Church cannot backed by Nazi. Church is for Christian and Semitic. Key is bright, just raise up the Church to higher platform. Simply as that.

Hence, Church alone is Government.

Yes alone. A Good Church is high mercy.

So same to the Administration. You got I meant.

False Algorithm, and false mind set. Rome tomorrow.

Its fun and its money. Correct me if I am wrong.
You know what.

My loyalty has dead end. I dont know how.

Someone is building the bridge, and someone is destroy it. And someone stay with crowd.

They doesn't know friendship. in which all love build on it, even the enemy is friendship too.

That about it too high level, I shall leave with me. The Wage issue again. And Allergy issue purely.

One harsh word, allergy!! forget about it. I declare this is not war but spiritual war against allergy of righteous.

Make love not make war. And I make war into love. Only King can do. More or less you too clever.

This is the Intelligence make you Winning.

How can it be done on War. I am help each other, find your root. It is in your pocket.
Sure thing is not your Name. Evil has no name.

Called them kings. Absolutely no place for you. Heaven has alot kings, and queens. But no King.

Which is no demand. something to earth.

No one to be king but billionaire. And all kings are billionaire. They are in pyramid bank.
Money From top to down. Flowing.

Head to the South, I issue the Warrant, the head is addressed and peace is coming. No more evil, as those evil bunches follow the head.

There are exceptional loophole of law. This is intentional protect the bastard. Forgive me bastard.

Not all bastard is bastard. But most. They are protecting church than other else. Some good some bad.

Once right is forever. I hope everybody understand, church is someone everything.
and everybody anything.

But those are bastard. Jesus protects people, he can build church in 3 days. And the step is protect family then Christian and Christian alike, so on. Leave Church alone.

Church has alot of funs and fund. That is a discovery of research. Doing conspiracy has no works at all.

So, Church very Rich and rich, and this fund flow into Someone account. Backed by Nazi.

I declare he is Nazi. And bunches of followers. This is someone happiness. My bullshit. There no time for evil, hence we shift to Protect the 3 people, elders, children, and women.

Salvation are random but Preaching is directional. Its freedom to choice. Its not business but life.

The Penalty of Wrong Preaching. Wrong theology. Let me think about it. 5 minute.

Girl B and Boy Sharp.

The whole story begin with the Panic of Conquer.

It was a raining day. And the sky is dark.

Road is clear.

The stomach is empty, and brain is faint.

The far side blinking the uncertain symbol.

Alot going to Pilgram, that is the 2nd year, 1st of May.

The chain linked up alot of memorandum.

Yes India Pilgram.
and no more.

The defeat of Israel is the Motive.

And Girl B and Boy Sharp is Nazi and Cult.

There is no Italy Mafia. This is a scam.

And Girl B and Boy Sharp is the Bethlehem.
and the Story end with the Boy A the Jordan.

Same story adapt from Biblical Science.
And this ruling the world.

This is the Big loop and the stair.
I cant tell you why.

How many people fallen because of this three character and Place.
Any one of you stay this place?

India the Pilgrim, Bethlehem the Marriage, and Jordan the Bank. And Girl B + Boy Sharp + Boy A.

This is an example of model story.

And from which it expanding into hybrid and hybrid. The Girl BB, and Boy B, Son E Flat.

The 3 Place upgrade into Thailand Picnic, London Bridge, Michael Page.

The Girl BB->Thailand Picnic, Boy B->London Bridge, and Son E Flat->Michael Page.

This is one of the major diaspora, of Y2k Bug since today.

The next is the most the important part. The axis is clear. The Family buy a bigger Flat.

Two Flat now, one big flat and one small flat.

so des ne. Its brothers.

the Son become into Christian.

The Two Flat is timed distance, even it is very near.

When Principle yield. When Son moves out from Parent, he will convert into Christian. And this family will extinct.

This Principle is famous Abraham Law.

The Rose is many. The Dark Rose is the God favourite.
And hence why the story end.

After many years..

The Two Flat become into a New Vatican. and the Dark Rose become into Bookmark.
The Fig tree has a name.

It is a number, 66.
Translated into English as 'Amen'.

So next time you hearing '66', this is going to Church.
and 6666 is going to Bank.

Thats the Distance from Bethlehem to Jordan.
The 6.3 Miles.

Where John the Baptist beheaded. That is the max the God can allow. And this is the Fire Baptism place too, what people sought after.

And Christmas is 6.3x2

or 12.4 more concise.

It is the improvised 6.4
The 12.4 a.k.a. Hill F.

This is the Ceremony day.

The resurrection day has plotted out.
The coming Christmas is the 74th.

Post. A.D. 74

There has never has a begin until Israel and Islam boundary pull apart.

This is the Weapon treaty zone. Gun control legislation highlighting.
No Bullet But alot Bulletin.

All are Chinese made Rocket.
You won't get hit.

The Pilgram zone is called as her name. When there is Christmas, there
Pilgram.
Distance from Jerusalem to Bethlehem and to Jordan are equal.

This is 9999 to 6666.

And This is the thing we can't change, and thing we can change.
1 Apollo is 3 Bachelor, and 1 Waterloo is 4 Make-low.

And everywhere make-low.

Because the Clock is White-Black-Yellow-Brown. Know the clock know the
place.

Its 1st and 1st and 1st.

This is sunday always.

The Head to the South. Hence, the Protest going. That the power comes.

Agree it or not, Skin is everything for my God. Join the crowd, join the crow.
The Big Boss no Castle.

No Faith at all for Crowd. And the Most Highly Place in the East.

Believe it or not. Castle has same kind gather. And the stone is charge by
ship cargo.
And when the world split, the semitic split.

The Solar Ether tells the Semitic is the Weakest and Fragile. The Semitic Flowers has the Answer. It drank Milk.

And this is the same description what about Semitic.

Man are not women. and women can be man.

Follow this golden rule.

What you eat important too. How you eat in proper way.

That deviate more higher ranking Supremacy.

Label and Pin are different application. Accumulated of pin is justice. accumulated label is penalty. giving justice, return with justice, same thing to penalty.

Whichever both undesirable.

Love penalty you freed. Love justice you wait.

Freedom make American Strong. Justice make Miracle and Tragedy. We have to confess.
Say no to Justice.

This is your pastor doesnt want you to know.

And welcome challenge. No justice, you live your own world. Its something we are not deserved but valuable.

The Job is easy, and worker has alot. When comes to penalty, it require win win.
Penalty is live within justice. Apology.

This just like Man and Women. Love is desirable. War is unavoidable.

When Man confront Man, it is peace forever.

Some people say, Man has end, and women doesnt. The Beginning of War is like that.
Next.

Next Slide.

The Platform is high, and Player are less.

What we after is Equality. The most deserved and desirable for each and everyone. This is represented by Money.

And Equality input and Equality output. So Equality split World into Groups. And Penalty split World into Love, Justice split World into War.

The Common Winner of these 3 is one group of people. This is none of other can copy.
It is the R rate.

Or no way.

When the platform get higher, there is repel. Renaissance is the thought, but When no equality is poverty.

And the edge of equality turns into bordered out. This Proprietary to owner use.
Something undesirable too.

All it takes is not Heritage of Ancestry, but Food more counted.

No meat.

And what differ the Marriage and Divorce is Brave and Brave.

Volume 4: Arrival of Galaxy of Autobot, the Mighty God had visit us, the Thy Kingdom has begun.

Man Made or God Made

Nazareth New Nativity Focus: From Footage Eden Garden to Universal Heaven

Christian Mathematics: Technology
Hybrid Engineering: Military Technology
Industrial Framework: Roll up Reynold Miller Constant

Y501. Christian Mathematics XI: Machine Computer Enclosure Reinvention to Knowledge Economy the Medicine (Whitepaper)

A. **Thermal Network UV 3G**, Moses Code (Stakeholder Version), Shepherd Dog, **IBM**
45.2 Latin Alphabet+7 Symbol, ISO Code
Linear Footage, All Module Network, Communication Products (Chronography)
Channel Network: Rulering
Tunnel the Web, profit index: Hosting Policy the Bandwidth Limiter
Poison Bill per Firewall Enclosure Subscription (Intellectual Foundation, e.g. Christian Treasure): Telecommunication Protocol the Algorithm Coverage
Gravitational Products: Sound Processing, e.g. Ant, Probe, Host, with Calendar Divisioning, the Stellar Ruler. e.g. Positioning Configuration and Numbers.
Thermal Products: Image Processing e.g. Ant, Probe, Host with Calendar Divisioning, the Quantum Ruler. e.g. Footage Calibration Test and Trials.

B. **Geothermal Network IR 1G**, Moses Code (Natalie Version), Goat, **Microsoft**
10 Universal Arabic Numbering
Discreet Footprint, All Analog Network, Circuit Products (Graded)
Client Network: Plotting
Program the Apps, profit index: 1R Correlation, 2R Solver, 3R Interfacing, 4R Simulation
Carbon Bill per Computer Program Footprint Mileage Licensed (Intelligence Ministry, e.g. News Centre): Simulation Reject Threshold
Module Products: Functional Heat Treatment, Automatic Series, Quantum Machine Roadmap
Toxic Bill per Calculator Program Testing Certified Fee (Bureau Ministry, e.g. History Research Initiative): Calendar Suit Schism, e.g. Eschatology Event or Islam Noel Event, Cult Caesar Event, Buddhism Ally Event etc.
Scalar Products: Algorithm Index Engine, Manual Generations, Stellar Machine Roadmap

C. **Antenna Network EMF 5G**, Moses Code (Intellect Version), Sheep, **Intel**
4 Holistic Roman Numbering
Arbitrary Histogram, All Digital Network, Diode Products (Pentecostal)
Server Network: Burning
Archived the Zip, profit index: Filler Plastic ROM, Alcohol Metallic Disc, Metallic Filler Disk, Filler the Paper
Nicotine Bill per Machine Cost Margin (Merchant Legacy, e.g. Security Trade): Universal Products: Plotter e.g. Cartridge Writer, Stellar Burner, Circuit Recorder

D. **Electrical Network ESD 3.5G**, Moses Code (Intelligence Version), Lamb, **Macintosh**

Greek Numbering

Footprint Histogram, All Scalar Network, Stellar Products (Benchmark)
Broadcast Network: Rating

Media the Logo, profit index: Communication Protocol, Carbon Copy the Cryptography

Hormone Bill per Credential Enclosure Charge (Secretary Platform, e.g. Trustworthy Channel): Cryptography Policy, Blind Carbon Copy the Calligraphy, **Motorised Products:** Printer e.g. Cartridge Ink Compressed, Stellar Ionised Air Compressed, Circuit Chemical Agent Compressed.

(Credit to "Grace Tan Shu Fen", Telecommunication Agent, College Bann list)

Y450. Christian Mathematics V: Chinese Royal Flush Calendar 锄大地日历法 (Whitepaper)

Holy Night, A.D. Year 1 | White Christmas, New B.C. Month 13 | Santa Claus Coming to Town, Post A.D. Day 1

500 Honey Years, **Land Footage** | 30 Salted Light Years, **Quantum Maturity** | 1000 Milky Years, **Gravity Grade**

End Loop, Hall Mark | Progress, Kelvin Mark | Program, Data Mark

5.1 **Zone Timer**, 5.1 Knot | 3.14 **Channel Resort**, 365Psi | **Space Footage**, 7.2G

Moses **Eucharistic Theory**, Homogenous | Gospel **Empirical Formula**, Holistic | Revelation **Constitution Law**, Orthogonal

Vision **Parametric Footage** by Nativity, sort out Critic | **Algorithm Maturity** by Calligraphy, sort out Schism| Cryptography by **Chronography Grade**, sort out Diaspora

RF Pasteurised Footage | IR Annealed Number | UV Tempered Grade

Genetic Dimension by **Time Footage** | Signal Transmit Frequency by **Heat Maturity** | Discrete Space by **Colour Grade**

Blueprint Projection Shoe | Blueprint Decryption Orthodox | Blueprint Cast Out Clan

4 Speed Rating, 4 Heat Flux Constant | 6.5 Heat Rating, 6.5 Magnetic Constant | 21 Quantum Number, 7.2 Gravity Constant

Texas Royal Flush | Chinese Royal flush | Omaha Royal Flush

Pilot, Advent | Automatic, Promised Land | Manual, Oriental

Copyright (C) 2022, Ryan Lai Hin Wai, All right reserved.

Y477. Christian Mathematics VIII: Croyals Version Industrial Revolution Framework to Rare Earth Economy the Metallurgy (Whitepaper)

A. Gold, Diamond: Discrete, 8cent, Silk
Aerial - 2D Einstein (Epsilon ε)
Computer Scheme – Data Core
Circuit Design
Telephone: Telecommunication Product -> Weapon Technology
Solar Dust Gun

B. White, Jade: No, dollar, Crystal
Holoscopic - 1D Newton (Alpha α)
Machine Scheme – Spectra Core
Material Design
Air Conditioner: Heat Exchanger Product -> Agriculture Technology
Solar Dust Timer

C. Blue, Sapphire: Wont, 3cent, Calcium
Orthogonal - 4D Archimedes (Lambda λ)
Pilot Scheme – Solver Core
Liquid Design
Television: Architectural Product -> Renaissance Technology
Quantum Paint

D. Pink, Pearl: Raised, free, Fur
Pentecostal - 6D Wesley (Omega Ω)
Calculator Scheme – Timer Core
Shield Design
Car: Informatic Product -> Medicine Technology
Remedy

E. Red, Ruby: Yes, 2cent, Skin
Holistic - 3D Solomon (Theta θ)
Modular Scheme – Energy Core
Carrier Design
Rocket: Enclosure Product -> Commuting Technology
Bio made Craft

F. Gland, Drug: Can, 1cent, Salt
Homogenous - 5D Bruce Lee (Psi ψ)
Navigation Scheme – Sensing Core
Lens Design
Camera: Erotic Product -> Entertainment Technology
Chronograph Camera

Y485. Christian Mathematics X: Croyalflush Standard Guidelines (Whitepaper)

I. Jobs - Croyals Version 石医版工业革命架构
Carrier Generations, C Number (Man Made)
Data Mark. National Heritage 国画, Chronography Age
Jacob's God: Lilith the Angel of Man
Fundamentalist, Non-Presbyterian, Christian Education, Ally to Buddhism

II. Ezra - Croyals Ecumenical Standard 石医版大公标准
Law Generations, Quantum Number (Auto Pilot)
Kelvin Mark, Flower Emblem 国花, Nativity Milestone
Noel's God: Serpent the Lord of Eden Garden
Puritan, Non-Methodist, Christian Ministry, Ally to Thither

III. Chronicle - Chinese Royal Flush Calendar 锄大地日历法
Dimension Generations, Greek Number (Pilot)
Gravity Mark, National Jewellery 国物, Cryptography Ranking
Abraham's God: The Lord of Semitic Passover
Apostolic, Non-Episcopal, God Ministry, Ally to Islam

IV. Exodus - Croyals Version Chinese Medicine Framework 石医版中医泛生架构
Footage Generations, R Number (God Made)
Hall Mark, National Animal 国宝, Ergonomic Standard
Adam's God: Jehovah the Image of God
Catholic, Non-Pentecostal, Doctrinal Training, Ally to New Age

A. Lent vs Critics: Nicotine Bill: Fee (Vulnerability)->Dollar (US)
Chips (e.g. Gambling) - **Organisation Holding** i.e. Address

B. Heritage vs Phantom: Hormone Bill: Credit (Accumulated)->Pound (UK)
Account (e.g. Gift) - **Aggregate Holding** i.e. Channel

C. Food vs Junk: Carbon Bill: Coupon (Scheme)->RMB (CN)
Pocket Money (e.g. Crime Disrupt) - **Foundation Holding** i.e. Pilgrim

D. Energy vs Schism: Poison Bill: Mileage (Solution)->Sterling (AU)
Bitcoin (e.g. Mining) - **Company Holding** i.e. Suit

Errata 26Dec2022

Y532. Christian Mathematics XIV: Stellar Science, Holistic Science, Stellarhood Science (Whitepaper)

A. **Stellar Science, Economic Framework,** Geothermal due Duty, Epsilon 光谱, Perfect Pitch

Lamb vs Tither vs Stakeholder vs Gentile, End Mileage

Aggregates of 8 Quantum Wave, and Conjugate of 9D, Quantum Track -> Netscape – Footage Miles End e.g. 8.9D

Tither Value: Tither Carrier to Destination, Netscape, Nativity

B. **Holistic Science, Medicine Framework,** Dynamics due Tither, Lambda 靠谱, Dated Pitch

Sheep vs Natalie vs Whitelist vs Antichrist, Dead End Miles

R Real Value, a.k.a. Quantum Number, i.e. Datum, Margin or Lock.
R Number is Footprint.
8 is Quantum Wave.
9 is Quantum Track.

C. **Stellarhood Science, Industrial Framework,** Kinematic due Lent, Sigma 不靠谱, Relative Pitch

Goat vs Intellect vs Think Tank vs Scapegoat, Sheppard Dog, No more Route

2D is 2 Axis
2.1D is 2Axis and Coring.
2.3D is 2Axis and 3 Coring.

Copyright (C) 2023, Ryan Lai Hin Wai, All right reserved.

Y558. Christian Mathematics XV: Telecommunication Defence Weapon Framework (Whitepaper)

I. Enclosure design, Lighting, Interior Design, Architectural, Land Scape, Town Planning Building.

II. Add on the Radiative Mounting i.e. Quantum inclined Planetary Machine, to Freed Preliminary from Disaster to Weapon Scam.

III. High Cost Battle Advantage to make Profitable, and Security Trade up.

Y594. Christian Mathematics XXII: Computer Core Evolution Framework, Protocol of 7.1 Adventist Church (Whitepaper)

"Once upon among the best but not the best"

A. Alternate Core: Stakeholder Whitelist, 4th Lambda, Original Heaven (99% Meta, Lost & Found Sheep, Coherent Signature Joshua)(Eschatology Calendar 8 Church/Chronicle 1 Church)

i. Philippians **(Texas Poker Suit, Nun or Sarah or E.T.)**(Holy See Church)/Colossians **(Omaha Poker Suit, Rabbi or Lilith or Unicorn)**(Orthogonal Church)/Ephesian **(Poker Tournament, Adam or Mary or Eve)**(Pentecostal Church)/Philemon **(Caribbean Poker Suit, Maria or Elizabeth or Michael)**(Charismatic Church) Epistle: Soul Mate Love Property Heritage of Heroin (Ancient Dragon, male)
1st Mission of Adventist True God Heaven: War & Wall for True God Kingdom to Come **(Abraham Transformer 3in1, Hebrew's Gothic vs Welsh/Adam Crab Machine 5per, Jewish's Roman vs Greek/Jacob Iron Man 4in1, Israelite's Chosen vs Chinese)**
ii. **UN: Fasci Socialist,** Public Army: FBI (Climate Protocol)**(Dollar, Blood or Cells)**
iii. Facebook: 1 met 1, many - any from many (Passover Post)
iv. IBM: Chronographer CPU, Dating Answer (3 in 1, Egg Benchmark)(Currency Packets), Transformer the Dimension Dust Filter
v. 20 Meta Capita Head = Selected Nationalist Church (High Intellect Capita)(Fasci Stellar Head to Fellowship the Jihad Pilgrim, Coherent Hall Mark)

B. Extra Core: Doer Blacklist, 7th Sigma, Fox Heaven (25% Meta, Goat, Inaugural Sealed Nazareth)(Biblical Etymology/Self-Anointed Identity)

i. Jude **(Wendy Suit, Chang'er the Rohs)** Epistle: Romance Love Miracle Healing of Justified Holy Spirit (Lion, male)
6th Mission of Herald Renaissance Heaven: Exit the Spiritual World, Filtered out True Biblical Enemy.
ii. **NATO: Nazi Communist,** Royal Army: Zion (Hygienic Policy)**(Won, Weapon or Treaty)**
iii. MIRC: 1 met 1, many - any from many (Watched Post)
iv. Chrome: Quantum Calibrator Android APU, AI (4per, Cola Benchmark), Chang'er the AI Machine
v. 22 Meta Capita Head = Selected Global Class Union (Low Intellect Capita)(Fasci Stellar Head to Grace Alone the Meta Licenses, Inaugural Kelvin Mark)

C. Alternate Loop: Stakeholder Blacklist, 666 Sigma Scapegoat (Lion Offspring, 7 per Sealed Jesuit)(1% Meta Sheppard Dog)(Nativity Consensus/Biblical Villain Clan)

i. Titus **(Chinese Poker Suit, Chris the President)** Epistle: Liberal Love Intellectual Heritage of Egoism (Dog, female)
2nd Mission of Oriental Heaven: War & Wall the Realism Land of Ancestry Treasure.

ii. **WWF: ISIS Computer Congress:** World Bank, Intellect Investment linked (Carbon/Dust Bill)**(Token, Leaf or Fruit)**

iii. Skype: 1 met 1, From many to many (Delayed Post)

iv. Microsoft: Metrology VPU, VR (5per, Polar Benchmark)(Heritage Aged), Crab Machine the Calligraphy Robot

v. 6 Meta Capita Head = Selected Secret Garden Family (Niched Biblical Capita)(Holy Spirit in Fellowship the Islam Pilgrim, 7per Hall Mark)

D. Extra Loop: Doer Whitelist, 13th Lambda Antichrist (Dragon Offspring, Final Signatured Chris)(75% Meta, Sheep)

i. Galatians **(Labour Suit, Apollo the Astronaut)** Epistle = Agape Love Miracle Binding of Glorified Holy Spirit (Sheep, female)
5th Mission of Parallel World the Utopia: Exit the Parallel World, True Inheritor by Wall & War Legalised Ancestry Treasure.

ii. **KMT: Fasci Mafia:** Tither Army: CIA (Hormones/Dust Bill)**(Sterling, Love or Bread)**

iii. ICQ: 1 met 1, From many to many (Instant Post)

iv. Pineapple II i.e. Durian: Thermal Miner VPU AR (4 in 2 core, Footprint Benchmark), Commuter Boxup the Metrology Satellite

v. 100 Meta Capita Head = Selected International Foundation & Agency (Generic Biblical Capita)(Holy Spirit in Grace Alone the Meta Atonement, Final Kelvin Mark)

E. Graded Loop: Think tank Blacklist, 7th Epsilon (1 Risen Meta, Lamb, 1st Flagship James)(Book of Life/12 Fruits Tree)

i. Hebrew **(Cowboy Suit, Kingkong the Mafia Leader)** Epistle = Pluto Miracle Partitionised of True Love (Unicorn, male)
3rd Mission of Renaissance Milestone Heaven: War & Wall the Authentic Land of True Love

ii. **NASA: Nazi Mafia:** Public Agency, Swiss Bank, Semitic Security Linked (Weapon Treaty)**(Grand, Bytes or Burn)**

iii. Twitter: any from many – any from many (Random Post)
Huawei, Power Hub: Scalar Solver, Bios Calibrate (5 in 1, Meta Overclock), Silicon Made (i.e. Quantum Cast Out), Carrier Commuter Teleport, the Heat Enclosure

iv. Huawei, Porting Hub: Universal Device, Modular Extension, Porting (5 in 1, Meta Regulator)(Capita Power), Commuting UFO Easter Bomb, the Light Enclosure

v. 200 Meta Capita Head = Selected Universal Christian Congress (Low Issued Meta Capita)(Holy Spirit in Spiritual Salvation the Official Redemption, 1st Conjugated Data Mark)

F. Graded Core: Thinktank Whitelist, 101per Epsilon (Unicorn Offspring, Original Flagship Messi)(6 Fallen Meta, Gentile)(101th Chopped/10 Heavenly Kings)

i. Corinthians **(Business Suit, Wisery the Architect)** Epistle = Holiness Miracle Resurrection of Holiness Love (Animal, female)
4th Mission of Utopia Beta Heaven: Exit the Dream by Seeking the True Love

ii. **WHO: Qing Organised Mafia:** Royal Agency, IMF Bank, Natalie Security Linked (Toxic/Dust Bill)**(Pound, Fabricate or Brick)**

iii. LinkedIn: any from many – any from many (Controlled Post)

iv. Macintosh: Cryptographer GPU, AR (4 in 1, Quantum Regulator), Commuting Iron Man the Pentecostal Instrument

v. 200 Meta Capita Head = Selected Multi-National Company (High Issued Capita)(Fasci Stellar Head in Spiritual Salvation the Free Invitation, Original Data Mark)

Errata 19Feb2023

Y480. Christian Mathematics IX: Quantum Number & Moses Law (Whitepaper)

Quantum 1: The Foundation for Beginner – Greedy, Social Bonding, Freedom

Quantum 2: The Pillar for Beginner – Economy, Semitic

Quantum 3: The Platform for Beginner – Covenant of Nuclear, Climate, Hygienic

Quantum 4: The Legacy for Beginner – Meta Concept, Theology, Genealogy, Stellar-logy, Chronography, Time Space Cryptography, Protocol Legislation, Voicing Practise etc.

Quantum 5: The Fundamental for Beginner – Biblical, Holistical, Chronicle

Quantum 6: The Principle for Medicine – DNA informatic, Allergy Grouping, Remedy Creation

Quantum 7: The Law for Social – Hierarchy, Montage, Meta, Carrier, Burden

Quantum 8: The Theory for Universe – Number of Axis, Elements, Singularity, Evolution, Reaction, Address Cryptography, Spectra Telescoping

Quantum 9: The Experimental for all Pentecost

Quantum 10: The Solution for Psychology

Quantum 11: The Solver for all Footage

Quantum 12: The Theorem for Universe

Quantum 13: The Act for Social

Quantum 14: The Covenant for War

Quantum 15: The Pillar for Advanced Learner

Quantum 16: The Platform for Advanced Learner

Quantum 17: The Legacy for Advanced Learner

Quantum 18: The Fundamental for Scorer

Quantum 19: The Legacy for Scorer

Quantum 20: The Platform for Scorer

Quantum 21: The Pillar for Scorer

*The Number of Iteration of folds, corresponding to Number of Carrier Element.
*a.k.a. Defect e.g. Warp Mark

Y366. Hybrid Engineering Part 1: Energy Driven Machine (Whitepaper)

Modular Machine vs Scalar Machine, Sort of debate continues.

In regard two type of Industry, the Automated and the Manual in which point to Perpetual Energy conservative rules. Gas Turbine is abuse of Energy, In compare Chemistry Energy, in which the Dark energy harvested from Brain instead, the famous Meta Energy.

This is about Holistic Design vs Up to date Blueprint Design. My 2 cents.

And all come from God made Holistic convert into Man Made Replica.

The Golden rule is, try Man Made. e.g. Token Machine Design.

Y367. Hybrid Engineering Part 2: Hybrid Machine & Computer (Whitepaper)

Hybrid is about Meta Law. Hence, Hybrid apply into Machine & Computer become Four Kind of Products, namely,

A. Smart Machine a.k.a. AI, VR, AR Machine and Efficient Thermal System a.k.a. Clean Energy System

B. Floating a.k.a. Electro Floating and Teleport Machine

C. Robot Computer a.k.a. Robot and Central Control System

D. Smart Structure a.k.a. Transformer and Robotic Arm

Copyright (C) 2022, Ryan Lai Hin Wai, All right reserved.

Y373. Hybrid Engineering Part 3: Four Kind Of Energy Theorem (Whitepaper)

A. Realism 真实: Non Meta 感觉 (tempo, timing), Universal Science, Esther
B. Fictional 虚构: Meta 画面 & Psycho 法则 (melody, climate), Popular Science, Newton
C. Possession 存在: Pseudo 理论 & Non Meta 感觉 (chord, temperature), Holistic Science, Einstein
D. Submission 泛滥: Psycho 法则 (rhythm, pressure), Discovery Science, Tesla

Y374. Hybrid Engineering Part 4: Anti Gravitational Energy (Whitepaper)

Water sectoring effect, the super high temperature induced anti gravitational energy.

Water 水: 硬水, 软水 Distil or Mineral

Same quantity of moles, but different subsidue compound.

The sectoring effect, due to the resonant mode. Not frequency but material properties combine with structural configuration.

Hence, the cup size could determined the Distil or Mineral.

Translate to Lake, River, Sea and Spring. The structure configuration also can be derived into tube configuration.

The applications of these include, heat sensor, heat pump. The anti gravitational energy harvest from super high temperature metal.

This material included calcium the highest ion carbon isotope. And belong to active heavy metal categories.

Heating of radiative metal could yield anti gravitational force. Vice verse.

Cooling of radiative metal could harvest free energy.

For anti gravitational is air floating, an unaccountable force. It is can not be a fatal weapon but an air condition machine. I meant. For long term it is a free energy too.

Copyright (C) 2022, Ryan Lai Hin Wai, All right reserved.

Y424. Golden Law of Energy and Food (Forum)

Democracy has 2 endevours. 1st, Diminished the Cult. 2nd, Diminished the Mafia. Its belief the Genocide is within Communist instead of Western as the Politic maturity is young.

What facing Asia is not Job Security. Again proven in series of Economic conspiracy against the Semiconductor Maker Economic Premises.

Thanks for God helping. That is false Moves of them. Its turn out Asia able to survive in Globalization.

Jew Community, yes only Canaan are Strengthen and Fortify. Not Spotify. How can it be done?

That is from avoiding the False Christianity Teaching. That the effort of Communist Chinese. Surprisingly they are against Cult.

Its now naming as Republican Chinese. and oversea Chinese was the Bait. They are in poisoned. extended to oversea Chinese.

There are App, Client, and Port. Clear your port, clear your ass. The best I can do.
The Port 78. This is Earth Science.

The Forbidden of Lead Frog. The ISIS. Steve Job. The RPG games. The Multi Talented. To Guard the Duty is not an easy thing.

And the Time can prove the duty. When they is Role Rotation, the player group will be changed too.

There are 50 port in total. The 50 Hierarchy Network. Which could form up alot of Channel by Bandwidth.

And yielding 10 Port only, by Frequency. The 10 Division, to be more precise. So probing the mainstream port. They could mix with alot good bandwidth channel. Said Facebook.
So technically is possible to diminished bandwidth.

As quantum can be gauged now. Its within numbers. Max of 9. So Who things moves upward. Called The New Platform.

Each milestone is about 5-40 years. What define milestone is energy packet. That make AI Vision. AI must be Banned. It is Full of Bugs. Mainly due to Automatic.
And no 2nd pillar of correlation.

One run in 5G. One run in 6G. The must be supplement with Rare Earth. What make different is the Clock Timing. And, that is about Meta and Meta Daily.

So if we can gauge the Humidity accurately. We can passed the Bios Test the Clock Timing gauge.

It of course must be scaled. We could simulated all in Computer. There are no alot of rules.

The Metallurgy is the bottleneck. 4 times right. What failed is the Timing Tax. Dont eat sandwich. Eat burger.

This is called Food Economy, that trouble Christian. We eat delicious only. The Food myth is within the Poison. My mother said.

So Processed Food Industry is a Subsidy Business. Same thing analogy to Vegetables.
From Harvest from Farming, the Climate is healthy.

Its good become better, and bad better lesser. This is the Assurance, when they is opposite, that must be temporary.

The Progression of 6 division. The insight behind of 38 line of Korea and North Korea. Its a variation the next.

When there is no Job security worrying, then we move to Social Security. Or Public Security?

Morons...There is ridiculous. Quantum claimed back. What worrying is the Islam Prophet. This is remarkable confidential information.

I meant the Islam Kingdom not Islam State. The Islam Kingdom is a hierarchy community.

It mixed with Syria, Kuwait, and Lebanon. etc. To accommodate the large population, the system is evil oriented priority.

One major Prophet and one minor prophet. That is ruling the Constitution, the Think Tank. as well as Lawmaker the navigator.

Of course, I particular with the Islam States only. Full bet on Islam State is Terrorism Scapegoat.

The Full Immunity Scapegoat. This differential out the Islam State from Islam Kingdom.
All Islam Prophet and Scholar are vulnerable to be Assassination. Not Politician Islam.
The true Image of Evil.

You cant hold this. It is Evil. It has no faith at all, all of them. The Church teach Mathematics. We are not God. We are Kings, and Jacks.

Mathematics without Church is Placebo Science. And you cant prophecy, if you in danger.

The Beauty and the Beast theory. When there is torture there is Holy spirit. There is for boosting.

For barbarian no knowledge of bible teaching. In Biblical, Holy Spirit is gained by Score, and Buying. a.k.a. Atonement and Redemption separately.

When the Score is low, better save up. Two Quantum Vision. That is called Chromatic Flush. The timing make difference.

The Hue make it vibrant, vivid, creamy. When you have quantum vision. I meant equip with quantum vision eyeglass.

With more camera formation, could capture time projected picture. It could used as Timing Teller, by capture Humidity at nano scaled.

Make Business more edge, make Social more Structure. That why business merge. That the Secret of many IT com. Secret to many IT com too.

The Emotionless Strategy. If you are startup. To prevent from take down, is to maintain hierarchy, not rewards.

The take down is very serious in IT Business since early days. Due to High Level Content and Public Visitor.

Elect the best and main positive competition is prevent IT world Genocide. IT world has too many victim, I reckon.

And there is last final step. To every American Business I reckon. This is the Hijack.
Blackmail??

Every Christian has two Shield. One is Genetic, one is Past Life. Best Bet is favour to Every Christian.

What temporary is costing. And That is follow the Closed not follow the Meta and Meta Dairy.

A Good Company is Auto Pilot. When the Country or Company on track, it meant the Economy and Wealth is on the slow transition.

This is the keyhold of 75 percentile theory. When that on track, the milestone has done simultaneously. Because of Fish Liked.

Its just called junction 8. When they has issue on maintain the 75 percentile theory. The problem must be the standard.

Ethnic is just Arbitrary. Precisely is the technique only. So the Standard meant Family and Community Cluster as well as Community Network small percentage.

That how the Wealth Heritage portfolio of previous Politic Regime. So the this population determine the World Heritage by Score and Exchange at inverted way.

There theorem of give and discount, at momentum way. So make the stream of heritage laminar.

Spiritual Boom could be killing than real bomb. Its man made community by charismatic. Same pattern.

The Islam State I reckon. Few times of Rotations. My friend call them RPG. This is Magical.

5 lens is the Keyhold. When you has the venue and latitude etc. you can spot people.
Make this Technology Commercial please.

It cannot used on timing duration, as timing has tax. But only Timeframe gauge.
God made and man made are difference.

The God doesnt make Land Mine. God made Roulette Pistol. Golden Rule, dont play with Timing kinda.

Time can killing people. Make you bend. Time itself is bomb. Spiritual Bomb is time bomb. When that occur is running of time.

Time can run, man cannot run. When there is running man, there is Truman. My stance is clear, the World must be Liberalised at bass fortify, then Internationalised together Globalised, that all.

When there is Satan, the Fundamental Law could loophole. That could lead you to fantasy or Wizard of Oz.

When there is No Room for Law Frauding, that could Islam Prayer did magical. Hence, that is costly and placebo. Don't worry. Be great.

When everybody right, then 100% guarantee escort. You will inheritance of Heritage from/in Heaven.

2nd clause, is to meet the 50% percentile population. By 2 parallel way, score and exchange. The mainstream by score, and Christian by exchange.

That include reject christian christian. Let show your muscle. So those poverty are those non Commonsense Religion.

Eating Vegetable? Mental Music Training? Tinitus? School Test? Army Test? Islam has new brainstorming.

No to test thing for selection. In Singapore, they called in Streaming.

Ultimately should be Monetary Control. The Power of God is mere of this. So when all this is right, we should be on the way it goes.

Yes, the background is condemn. Christmas count down. From Top to bottom.
From Mining rich country is remote country.

Due to the Spiritual Rich. No climate issue. That is comfort zone instead. And the least is the Crude Oil Rich Country.

Precisely this tells about the Geothermal and Genetic only. The Free play is limited to Cryptography Identity.

50 Hierarchy. The World Meta. For example Labour. And Military the highest. Highest mean identity, lowest mean identical.

So this determine the Remote Country and City Country. The China University teaching in past decade.

The Traffic University. Alot. All begin with with Bicycle. What their big plan? The calling of Son of Dragon.

We have conquer Climate Change, and Social Population Chaos. But all build on soft rock.

The Political Evolution and Naming system. Meaning political evolution determine the Maturity of Spiritual.

Meaning Information mass media has too little. This filtered out alot of evil. Free Mass Media is Terrorism.

Terrorism Government Hijack Righteous Government. Politic is a money game.
Low Pay Politician has alot.

Terrorism is about Religion Benefit. The Hell Religion. Make Paradise become Hell.
Hell mean Identical.

When the country is temporary, it mean hell. Or heaven like wise. There is only Temporary Terrorism Benefit.

It cost alot to maintain, particular to Spiritual Rich Country. In most asia Country, we called it Martial Act.

To personal also same. In ancient all the way until modern day. Called it Lock Tradezone. Feudal system.

That the Fight against the Postpone Heaven Organisation. Take the earliest Flight, let those dead bury the dead.

Just entertainment, no for high blood pressure. Don't ask people join you. If you are Islam, don't ask Christian Convert.

We are upgrading progressively whole world. No country left behind. Those remain third world is Anti Semitic closure.

You couldnt name alot. I meant it is building castle in the sky. A New World Indeed called Third World.

By Meta Science, all Heritage should be Culture. No fashion. That is for Actor. Most Celebrity has moderate Wealth, because of Duty a nd Levy.

The Levy and Duty could put you in jail, in ancient. Democracy is for terrorism, and hence politician are safe.

Sound correct, but no commonsense. There are 2 kind Democracy, the Begin with diminished Cult and Ending with diminished Mafia.

Wrong side makes double action. The Democrat Capitalist, and Democract Socialist the one cope with Think Tank.

Its Liberal after all, all politic is game. That why control politic is not for goal is for score.
Its for education.

I still adapt Martial Act, when crisis. When you have less connnection, you have more shield. Vice verse. All are fake one.

That is Christology theology. The Christ Church teaching. Its more or less compare to Mainstream.

When the time reached, whole world become floated. Not suprise, that the Gold mining.
ESD could proven. The Gold Provide the Stiff Job.

Lets Make a Conclusion on the Terrorism Battle. The Insight tells its could be Active or Passive. Dont Panic.

Whatever, Active or Passive. Both point toward Religion Benefit. That is the Insight Tellers. Say Islam Democrats and Charismatic Wave Champaign.

Marxist Communist is Nazi hideout, and belief linked with Terrorism. This is abit Variation, as Marxist Communist China, is belong to Mao Zhedong Politic Idealogy not Karl Marx Politic Idealogy. Building on different Foundation on Marriage Act.

Marriage Theory of Fish. Those Fish Theory inclined are those to Change the Heaven and Earth upside down. These apparently can seen from the 50 Land Communities.
You Win some you lose some.

Does Heaven Heritage vulnerable from Terrorism? Let make a good deal. When people losing Justice, terrorism is the keyhold.

Let's justice be quick. People thought War is justice, in fact this is undeniable. But We are no more barbarian to fight the War.

So End Terrorism and End the War, End Everything. Start Free Speech which is good.
Words is Build, War is destroy, Terrorism is hiding.

When Business Merge, it losing more. Democracy is localisation. a.k.a. Liberalisation.
So Islam State form (Sri Lanka), China Oriental Democracy forms (Hongkong). Both are Terrorism.

This is for Religion Benefit, The Islam State join with Charismatic forms Womanized Society.

This is a Homogeneous Society. One Leader. Precisely, One Iconic Leader. It has to be that way, people said Dalai Lama. Maybe Next.

Who grab the stick, who has the iconic Spiritual. I don't know how many generation now.

So Those Church Serving False Pentecost Ministry called False Spirit. And those Islam serving the Pentecost Ministry.

The Babel Tower. What Christian Do, Islam Cannot Do. They are God breed. And Christian Has Alot Levy.

Let's facing the benefit that God giving. All has gift, just blind faith for those low power. The least is the greatest in Fashion Society. This is norms.

This is the scam to join the big group evil. When the Society growth Large, it become bottom ranking.

And that could become the top either. If it is God Breed Ethnic. Heritage thief become topic now.

We Christian are Christ Breed. Or Jesus breed. This list out Energy & Food Heritage and Blueprint & Culture Heritage.

Once you got the Treasure of Blueprint. Everything just cast out. This make up Christian Organisation in future.

To less Workers. Culture is the Opposite to Blueprint, it is suppose to Projected out into Every Humanity Records, a Museum Retro.

Talk about Food, Japanese and Korea Food is most Profitable. Indian and African Food also Profitable. Not Kebab.

There rest called Christian Food, Fine Dining. For Passionate Chef. Chinese Hawker food has poison.

Same thing apply to Combustion, Reactor, Generator, and Fuel Cell. These Energy Heritage is immediate availability to Islam Country, due to Bottleneck of Nuclear Treaty.

As Nuclear Treaty is toward Christian Country. When talk about environment protection, Christian Country has alot of Regulation to meet.

But not Islam Country as their product sell to Middle East. This make Energy expensive Bill to West and China, same same. All from Royalism Concept.

Mistake comes with Free Lesson. Nobody do energy better than American. "Go is a must, and there is U turn". Soldier Attitude. Just procedure.

They good job are those no levy.

Glossary

1. The Economy & Politic (Jerusalem Foundation)

Timeline of end world: Zigzac, and anytime.

Mastermind: Racist related, not money related for sure.

Marriage Supremacy: Non Specific Marriage, preferential on Bread over Love. Advocate Testimony.

Marriage Autonomy: Specific Marriage, preferential on Love over Bread. Advocate Ministry.

Political Wing: Far left point to conservative, far right point to radical.

Superstitious: Crime Disorder, Erotic, Heresy, Multi-theism, e.g. Crime.

Idealism: Economy Disorder, Idealism, Serve two God, Trinit-ism e.g. Terrorism.

Materialism: Social Disorder, Secular, No Righteous, Monotheism, e.g. Raping.

Popularism: Civil Disorder, Nationalism, Idolism, Agnostic, e.g. Fraud.

Marxism: Marxism, Far Left wing, Socialism.

Fusionism: Fusionism, Centre Left wing, Religionism.

Nazism: Far Right wing, Materialism.

Fascism: Fascism, Centre Right wing, Racialism.

Neo Nazi: Economy Disorder as well as Anti-Chinese. Enterprise Syndicate incl. Qing Syndicate. Anti-Chinese.

Fasci Japan: Civil Disorder as well as Anti-God. Crime Syndicate incl. East India Company. Qing Regime.

Nazi Germany: Social Disorder as well as Anti-Semitic. War Syndicate. Anti-Semitic. Soong Sister Dynasty.

Communist Crime Disorder as well as Anti-Christ. Terrorism Syndicate incl. Islamic State. Qing Conspiracy Basement.

Russian Bratva: Linkup to Taliban & Mind Control Society. Custom Committee.

East India Company: Linkup to Al-Qaeda & Casino Society. Hospital Committee.

Klu Klux Klan: Linkup to ISIS & Mental Research Institute. Casino Committee.

Italy Mafia: Linkup to Islamic State & Falungong syndicate. Bank Committee.

IQ: Intelligence Quotient, Identity, Statistical.

AQ: Adversity Quotient, Thing, Parameter.

CQ: Creative Quotient, Time, Directional.

EQ: Emotional Quotient, Place, Geometrical.

Goal Oriented: Two-way thinking. Versus analysis. Duality.

Task Oriented: Alternative way thinking. Brainstorming. One direction.

Result Oriented: Multiple-way thinking. Independent analysis. Concurrent.

Process Oriented: One-way thinking. Critical analysis. Sequence.

Nationalism: Three party formation a.k.a. 3 People's Principle. Human Right inclined. e.g. Protestation.

Pan Democracy: Alliance formation, Coverage inclined. e.g. Money Campaign.

Democracy: Coalition formation, Two party political formation. Credit Inclined. e.g. Presidential Election.

Republican: One party formation. Population inclined. e.g. General Election.

Federalism: Slaved & Commercial Crime inclined. Charity model. Government Monetary.

Commonwealth: Erotic & Intelligence Crime inclined, Labour inclined. Investment model. Family Monetary.

Capitalism: Labour & Criminal Crime inclined. Supply Chain model. Individual Monetary.

Communism: Servicing & Civil Crime, Servicing inclined. Franchised model. Partial Government Monetary.

Reunification of Religion: Oppose to Renaissance. Religion Unity. Economy Recession. Shia Islam commission, e.g. Babylon.

Economics transformation: Oppose Industrial Revolution. Economy Booming. Agnostic Islam commission, e.g. Nile River.

Cultural Renaissance: Belong to Social Disorder. No racial discrimination and racial reconciliation but Anti-Semitic. Economy Downturn. Sufism Islam commission, e.g. Aegean Sea.

Industrial Revolution: Technology foundation as well as infrastructure upgrading. Economy Crisis. Sunni Islam commission, e.g. Babel Tower.

Continue on Next Page

1a. Published (Croyalflush Ministry Foundation 锄大地事工基金会)

Socialist: Think Tank->Antichrist
Non Socialist: Fund->Gentile
Democratic: Scapegoat->Biblical Villain
Politic: Psychology->Edge
Religion: Criminology->Credit

Annealed (Metallurgy Terms): To make Holistic, grouped-out by same properties.
Tempered (Metallurgy Terms): To make Cluster, grouped-in by different properties.
Pasteurised (Pharmacy Terms): To make Homogenous, grouped-in by different properties.
Sterilized (Pharmacy Terms): To make Network, grouped-in by same properties.
Premise: Technology Heritage, gauged by Patent.
State: Culture Heritage, gauged by Copyright.
Nation: Humanity Heritage, gauged by Service Mark.
Kingdom: Property Heritage, gauged by Trade Secret.
Holy Spirit: Greater than 3 out of 6 Division Social Maturity. The Cold inclined Annealed Communities.
Evil Spirit: Lower than 3 out of 6 Division Social Maturity. The Hot inclined Pasteurised Communities.
Annealed Community: Social Bonding Ethnic, e.g. 1st. Israelite, 2nd. Germanic 3rd. Celt,. Diaspora. Goat. Many.
Tempered Community: Social Chaos Ethnic, e.g. 1st. Jewish, 2nd. Chinese/Asian, e.g. Aboriginal, Lamb. Unique.
Pasteurised Community: Social Disorder Ethnic, Jew/Germans, Anglo/Jew, e.g. Indigenous. Sheep. Large.
Sterilised Community: Social Order Ethnic, e.g. 1. Turkish, 2. Egyptian, 3. Arabian, 4. Persian, 5. African. Gentile. Uniform.
Nationalist: Pasteurised Community.
Socialist: Tempered Community.
Democracy: Annealed Community.
Republican: Sterilised Community.
Globalisation: Make 5 Axis Heritage, a.k.a. Economic Harvest. 50 milestone.
Internationalisation: Make 4 Axis Heritage, a.k.a. Economic Myth. 30 milestone.
Liberalisation: Make 3 Axis Heritage, a.k.a. Economic Booming. 40 milestone.
Cryptography: Identity Verification Method.
Guarantee: The Amount of Credit Projected in Time or Volume, equivalent to Liability.
Ante: The Amount of Credit equivalent to Partial of Liability.
Guarantor: The Identity or Represented Organisation equivalent to Partial of Liability.

Extremist Christian: Social Disorder
Lyrics Music: Calligraphy Music
Data Mark Geology: Tempered Zone, Safe Environment Zone a.k.a. First Resort
Kelvin Mark Geography: Annealed Zone, Safe Spiritual a.k.a. Second Resort
Hall Mark Demography: Pasteurised Zone, Safe Time Zone a.k.a. Last Resort

Community Hierarchy: A.D. and New A.D.
Ethnic Hierarchy: B.C. and New B.C.
Clan: First Resort, Blueprint Cast out, Chronography e.g. Pluto
Schism: Second Resort, Blueprint Decryption, Calligraphy e.g. Heresy
Shoe: Last Resort, Blueprint Projection, Nativity, e.g. Critics

Duty Exception per Capita: Identity
Tax Legislation: Bureau
Identity per Calendar Lapsed: Misconduction Degree
Identity per Calendar: Seal Number the Ethnic
Type of Calendar: Seal Event per Religion
High Seal Number: Heavy Bureau Tax

Bureau Tax: Capita Volume the Population Census
Bureau Organisation: Promote Religion Unity the Extreme Islam
Crime Disruption Ministry: War Organisation and Crime Organisation.

Military Regime: Continent per Capita
Politician Party: Cryptography per Capita
Bi-Parliament: Career Selection
Hierarchy Parliament: Career Founder, per Capita
Nationalist: Laboratory e.g. Science Data Analysis
Democracy: Office e.g. Technology Development
Fasci Socialist: Church e.g. Ecumenical Standard Initiative, the Judification
Marxism Socialist: University e.g. Engineering Standard Initiative, the Framework

Private Mail: Intelligence + Broadcast i.e. CCC
Public Published: Meta Tither + Broadcast i.e. Real Value
Fashion Big Ante: Commuting + Meta Tither i.e. Truth Value

Continue on Next Page

2. The Ethnicity & Business (World Bank)

Jew 3 tribes: Zion i.e. Irish, Hebrew i.e. Jew, Semitic i.e. Jude.

Semitic 12 sects: Any ethnic pre-selection for salvation among each racial formed the definition of Semitic 12 sects. e.g. Israel, Hongkong, Dubai, New Delphi, total 12 sects.

Copyright: Foundation, Improvised version.

Patent: Pillar, Authentic version.

Copycat: Platform, Ugly version.

Trademark: Legacy, Beautified version.

Service Mark: Fundamental, Draft version.

Improvised: a.k.a. Jazz, Original Chord, Advertisement Music. incl. Poetry song.

Retro: a.k.a. Folk, Original Melody, Sheet Music. incl. Church song.

Indie: a.k.a. Pop, Original Tone, Album Music. incl. Christmas song.

Unplugged: a.k.a. Rock, Original Tempo, Concert Music. incl. Hymn song.

Classical: a.k.a. Symphony, Original Rhythm, Recording Music. incl. Praise song.

Dali 大理: Suspended Scale. Indian, Mainland Chinese 华夏民族, incl. 闽, 澳, 台

Dunhuang 敦煌: Harmonic Minor Scale. Chosen, Diaspora Chinese 中华民族, incl. 津, 港, 新

Shangri La 香格里拉: Diminished Scale. Korean, National Chinese 大汉民族, incl. 浙

Green Island 绿岛: Harmonic Major Scale. Japanese, Mandarin Chinese 大华民族, incl. 京, 苏, 粤

Dagger 小刀会: Augmented Scale. Thai, Oversea Chinese 华侨民族, incl. 桂, 蒙

Broadway: 1 per Bass, Portuguese incl. African, Portuguese

Quartet: 4 per Strings, Spanish incl. Jude, Greek, Spanish

Band: 3 per Choir, French incl. Germanic, Irish, French

Accompany: 2 per Piano, Dutch incl. Celt, Dutch

Orchestra: 5 per Drum, Italian incl. Jew, Italian

Boiled; Baked: Pork & Seafood, South America, Macao,Nanjing.

Steamed; Stew: Mutton & Venison, Europe, Taiwan,Tianjing.

Stir Fry; Roasted: Poultry & Vegetable, Australia, Malaysia,Shanghai.

Fried; Grill: Fish & Egg, United Kingdom, Hongkong,Beijing.

Braised; Gravy: Beef & Duck, United States, Singapore,Shenzhen

Chinese Medicine: Therapy e.g. Acupuncture.

Drug: Herbs e.g. Supplementary.

Vaccine: Cures e.g. Immune.

Pharmacy: Tonics e.g. Nutriology.

Quarantine Management: Testing e.g. Laboratory.

Regenerative Medicine: Chinese Medicine, New Age Medicine, Psychiatry Drug, Herbs, Therapy Oriented.

Nutriology Medicine: Western Medicine, Surgical Medicine, Pharmacy Supplement, Tonics, Anatomy Oriented.

Hexagram Code Numeric, Cipher, Superimposed, Chronicle to Name Etymology.
Morse Code Alphabet, String, Thread, Festival to Name Etymology.
Light Code Symbol, Echo, Histogram, Capital to Name Etymology.

Continue on Next Page

2a. Published (Chinese Reunion Fellowship 新中华府)

Blueprint: Practise, Theory, Model, (Data Mark, Kelvin Mark, Hall Mark).
Chronography: No Clan, Diaspora
Calligraphy: Non Orthodox, Schism
Nativity: No Shoe, Critic
Carrier: Best Treasure Ethnic
Pilot: Best Intellectual Ethnic
Treasure Integrity: Human Right Act
Intellectual Integrity: Intelligence Act

Food Scheme: Class A1: Tamed, Class F4: Seafood, Class C: Herb, Low<High Class: Mouse<Bird
Energy Scheme: Class A1: Hormone Bill, Class F4: Carbon Bill, Class C: Poison Bill, Low<High Class: Calories<Calcium Bill
Pentecost Legacy Scheme: Class A1: Wage Duty Carrier, Class F4: Compensation Duty Carrier, Class C: Salary Duty Carrier, Low<High Class: Devotion<Burden Duty Carrier, i.e. Cryptography
Meta Genetic Scheme: Class A1: Culture Renaissance, Class F4: Humanity Renaissance, Class C: Heritage Renaissance, Low<High Class: Industrial<Technology Renaissance, i.e. Nativity
Quantum Treasure Scheme: Class A1: Advent, Class F4: Oriental, Class C: Promised Land, Low<High Class: Utopia, i.e. Chronography
Esther: Star Dust Stream, Time tax
Ezra: Star Dust Pressure, Heat tax
Nehemiah: Star Dust Wind, Quantum tax
Economic Conspiracy: Christian Persecution. Third World. Junk Technology, a.k.a. Renaissance Era.
Heritage Terrorism: Anti Semitic. First World. Junk Culture, a.k.a. Contemporary Era.
Royalty: Depend on Geology, Space Footage, the Merchant Age. The Intelligence.
Loyalty: Depend on Geography, Spiritual Channel, the Marketing Standard. The Broadcast.
Lent: Depend on Demography, Time Zone, the Insurance Ranking. The Calculating.

Natalie: Clock Wise Meta, Class A1, 88 Graded Weighted Piano
Intellect: Anti Clock Wise Meta, Class C, Flute
Sheep: Anti Clock Wise Meta, Class B, Guitar
Goat: Clock Wise Meta, Class C, Violin
Lamb: Clock Wise Meta, Class B, Cello
Gentile: Clock Wise Meta, Class F4, Keyboard Piano

Lent Legislation Law: Lent, Loyalty, Royalty
Intelligence Fee: The Value counted from Tax of Duty whenever equilibrium.
Intelligence: Carrier Meta
Land Property Value: Footage Milestone per Boundary Datum

3. The Religion & Theology (Vatican Organisation)

Theorem: Business Management, Telecommunication, Pseudo Science; Commission.

Theory: a.k.a. Law, Astronomy, Arts, Applied Physics, Nature Science; Ethic.

Theology: a.k.a. Canon, Politics, Risk Management, Operation Management, Social Science; Spirit.

Doctrine: a.k.a. Principle, Medicine, Music, Logistic, Architecture Science; Ethnic.

Dogma: a.k.a. Theory, Martial Arts, War Strategic, Criminology, Psychology; Erotic.

Principle: Genealogy and Medicine. a.k.a. Bible Character. i.e. Ethnic.

Law: Archaeology and Astronomy. a.k.a. Bible Story i.e. Ethic.

Catechism: Constitutions and Politics. a.k.a. Canon of Bible.

Justice: Criminal Law and Anti-Social Law, against Crime Disorder i.e. Criminal Justification.

Justification: Holy Confession, Forgiveness, Faith, Speak in tongue.

Sanctification: Holy Baptism, Repentance, Love, Pentecost.

Glorification: Holy Communion, Offering, Hope, Theosis.

Regeneration: Holy Sacrament, Righteousness, Work, Christian Perfection.

Testimony: Its harms than benefit, do ministry than testimonial for Orthodox Christianity nor for Atheism.

Orthodox Christianity: Apostolic Church where Ministry of God as well as Missionary is valued. Teaching of Overview and strengthening of Christianity Fundamental.

Lutheran: Churches that value Salvation by Faith alone as well as value 'No racial discrimination', it is disrupting social harmony if too vigorous. Teaching of Basic and strengthening Christianity Foundation.

Christianity Reforming: Separating Lutheran Church out of four division of Christianity denomination.

Trinity: One to Three, Three entity regulated to Core.

Monotheism: Three in One, Three core regulated to one entity.

Erotic Defect: Man or women whoever compromise sex before and/or after marriage.

Adultery: Man or women pursuit love for money or pursuit love for sex before and/or after marriage.

Evil Spirit: Whoever contributing to social disorder as well as strong will of destruction conscious holistically.

Anti-Semitic: Link to Nazi Germany, in which any illegal activities contributed to disrupting Jew as well as those Pre-selection Jew from each racial group, for reconciliation.

Religion Unity: Link to Christianity Reforming, The endeavour of Orthodox Christianity to form alliance with Islam as well as other Orthodox religion.

Heaven: Link to Social Disorder, the place called itself heaven is the place where no social disorder and forward to progressive high civilisation and to perpetual life.

Christian Science: Conclude in Scientific theology as well as Creationism belief, a.k.a. Fundamentalist.

Pseudo Science: Conclude in Telecommunication as well as Revelation belief, a.k.a. Pentecostal.

Salvation: Those who are Completed Christian as well as those who equip with Christianity equivalent methodology. There are no single way but many way lead to salvation.

Canon: The rule in and rule out of targeted number of books from Old Testament as well as from New Testament to form an interconnected logical loops in other to fulfil the teachings of Salvation of Christ.

Climate Disaster Readiness: Conspiracy of Tsunami, targeting to block the evangelism of Christianity as well as targeting disrupt human civilisation by minimising the global emergency readiness in all activities to disperse human connection e.g. Social Disorder, Anti-Semitic, Religion disharmony, Terrorism, Erotic defect, World War.

Nuclear Weapon: High destructive, low occurrence nuclear weapon, literally it has no threatening advantage over other mass destructive weapon. But it can be illegally misused out of control the crude oil economy as well as preventive measure of escalating to World war.

Social Disorder: Link to Nazi Germany, in which a society harmony is disrupted in terms of social connection as well as social affiliation on weighing to leader of society.

Social Security: Liability on privacy/freedom that cause threat, depends on social sensitivity, popularism & social ranking mismatched i.e. social disorder.

Semitic Persecution: Social Disorder Activity, incl. Quarantine, Job sanction. Same to Christian Persecution.

Continue on Next Page

3a. Published (Christian Organisation 基督徒集团)

Goat: Intellect, Word Prison, Semitic
Sheep: Tither, Trojan Horse, Christian
Lamb: Natalie, Colony, Anointed

Scapegoat: Terrorism Ransom to Semitic, Memory Defect, Alternate Semitic
Antichrist: Chronic Failure Ransom to Christian, Erotic Defect, Extra Christian
Gentile: Disaster Ransom to Stakeholder, Poison Defect, Grading Reincarnated

101 Righteous Sheppard Dogs: Duty Ransom, Sigma, Lion
99 Lost and Found Sheeps: Threatening Lawsuit, Omega, Horse
500 Repel Lambs: Guinea Trial, Lambda, Dragon

Cult a.k.a. Oriental Democracy: Buddhism Noel, Christian Persecution, Democracy Academy, Alternate Camps
Communist a.k.a. Fasci Socialist: Utopia Series, Stakeholder Persecution, Royalism Military, Extra Censors
Islam Prayer a.k.a. Aqueda: Islam Noel, Semitic Persecution, Constitutional Congress, Grading Streams

Hierarchy Traitor: African, Nazi Fasci
Regime Repel: Jew, Mafia
Cells Schism: Manchu, Syndicate

Footage Binding: Capita Suit, Chronography
Cryptography Milestone: Capita Scheme, Calligraphy
Footprint Clock: Capita Clan, Demography

Redemption: Body Lapsed
Atonement: Spiritual Mileage
Judification: Fellowship Margin

Holistic Science: Biblical Conjugation
Pseudo Science: Mechanics Reaction
Systematic Science: Mechanics Mechanism

Montage Intellectual: Universal Spectrum Histogram
Social Montage: Political Evolutional Scheme
Social Hierarchy: Moses code Iteration number

Rabbi: Academy Scholarship, Queen the Inaugural
Puppet: Congress Stakeholder, King the Final
Idol: Market Moderator, Jack the Least

Meta Clock the Diaspora, Byte: Reactors Programs, the Clustered Stereotype,

Isomer, Timber Product Graded, i.e. Heat Flux
Timer Clock the Heat, Era: Mechanism Series, the Stereotype Bind
Number,
Isotope, Metal Element Trajectory, i.e. Heat Carrier
Sets of Clock the Voltage, Value: Mechanics Generations, the Genealogy
Wave,
Isometric, Silicon Energy Releasing, i.e. Lumen Value.

Chronicle: Eschatology Calendar Atonement Byte per Gross Capita a.k.a.
Ether Stellar i.e. Solar Stellar, the National Treasure, Hygienic the Tax
Agency. UN, WWF, KMT, World Bank. Publisher Certification Protocol
Jobs: Ecumenical Judification Era per Gross Capita a.k.a. Solar Wave, the
Universal Energy, Administration the Space Agency. NASA, WHO, NATO,
Vatican. Medicine Scheme Cover
Exodus: Industrial Framework Redemption Value per Capita a.k.a. Ether
Dust i.e. Solar Dust, the International Economy, Intelligence the Bureau
Agency. CIA, FBI, ZION, Jerusalem. Wage Deficit Package

Adventist or Eschatology Calendar: Covenant, Universal Sins Protocol e.g.
Etymology
Judification or Ecumenical Catechism: Doctrine, Constitutional Sets of
Law, e.g. Ecumenical
Economic Treasure or Etymology Semitic Congress: Dogma, Orthogonal,
Aerial, Pentecostal, Holoscopic, e.g. Holysee

Democracy: University
Royalism: Academy

Ritual: Quantum Carrier Metric. The Conversation Bill for Real Value.
Legitimated: Judification Platform. e.g. Platform Saving Account. Distrust
Account Platform. Allergy Account Platform. i.e. The Famous Ecumenical of
Vatican contrast with the HolySee.

Stellar Head: Community Leader and Spiritual Leader.
18 Luohan: The Fasci Community Leader of 18per. e.g. Pope, Bishop, Islam
Prophet or Islam Spiritual for Jihad, the Revenge.

Continue on Next Page

Continued

Federal per Capita: Spiritual Cast Out the Derivative Products due Misdoing and Perceiving-ness the Aggregate. Timely Kick out High Bonding Product. (The Commuting Generations)
Gross Capital per Clan: Marriage or Max Tither, Food Compound Profit Sharing Ranking (The Inaugural Sky High Nativity)
Nativity Mileage per Capita: Carrier Tither, Commuting Energy Cost (Land Wall)
Nativity Milestone per Gross Capital: Timezone any One to One Couple only, Homogenous, the Time Lock Metric (Eden Garden the Schematic to Next and Original, i.e. One Lord, Two Lord, Trinity Lord, and Multiple Lord, no more Lord)

Security Bank, Federal Bank: Option Security Branch and Trading Security Branch
Investment Bank, World Bank: Property Bonds Investment Branch and Labour Investment Branch

Sea, Harbour:
Dust, Axis Carrier Tither:
Meta Tither:

World of Renaissance to Oriental: Ban Civilisation of Humanity (i.e. Sky Community) in Marriage to Tither Marriage, Islam Ally
World of Herald to Adventist: Promote Civilisation of Culture (i.e. Land Community) in Tither Carrier to Fallacy to Distortion Carrier, Buddhism Ally

Sodomy: Pilgrim
Virginia: Anabaptism

Continue on Next Page

4. The Technology & Science (United Nations Agency)

Upstream technology: Fundamental/Innovative technology rely on academic.

Downstream technology: Foundation/Frontier technology rely on experiment.

Health Law: i.e. Systematic Biology a.k.a. Robot Technology, Hardware. 12 symbol, 12 Robot Organs as well as 12 Human Organs corresponding to 12 Chemistry Compound, incl. 3 Energy Mechanism.

Psychology Law: i.e. Systematic Psychology. a.k.a. Robot Technology, Software. Intelligence, Emotional, Creative and Adversity Quotient. incl. Scalar Computer, e.g. Measuring software, Quantum Computer, e.g. Solver software.

Pharmacy: Enzymes, Hormones, Mucosa, Insulin corresponding to Stem cell, Vitamin, Analgesic, Steroid.

Artificial Intelligence: Technology about Automation and Robot. If Civilisation reach peak, beyond that would bring humanity destruction, point to Medicine Science and Telecommunication Science.

Augmented Reality: Technology about Machine and Robotic. If Civilisation reach a stalled situation, above that would bring humanity advanced, point to Logistic Science and Combustion Science.

Virtual Reality: Technology about Simulation and Computer. If Civilisation reach crisis, below that would bring humanity downturn, point to Engineering and Computer Science.

Economy Load: Quantity of Mainstream Population, as High quantity of Mainstream population comes along reduced Economy Bill.

Mainstream population: The Bandwidth of telecommunication is the measure of Mainstream population.

Life expectancy: The measure of telecommunication bandwidth of a person, point to their endervour, ministry and life expectancy.

Harvest Gain Theory: i.e. Calendar Theory, a.k.a. Relativity Theory. The relationship of (Bandwidth of telecommunication)$^{\text{power of } X}$/(Half-life) proportional to (Harvest Gain). Analogy from Farmers and Fisherman. Half-life is a constant, but it depend on the gravitational field, i.e. moon phase. These contributed to Operation Management e.g. Agriculture, Food.

Chaos Theory: i.e. Time progression Theory, a.k.a. Entropy Theory, 2 way time progression, Closed form system, Predictable, Entropy, series events, Automatic Guiding, End loops, Analogy from Combustion Science. These contributed to Transportation e.g. Satellite, Jet.

Reality Decryption Theory: i.e. Augmented Reality Theory a.k.a. Feedback Control Theory, Algorithm Engine (Sensor, Encryptor) transfer to Combustion Engine (Actuator, Synthesizer) then to Film Engine (Gauge, Decryptor), Analogy from Computer Science. These contributed to Augmented Reality e.g. Mining, Construction, Nuclear Reactor etc.

Light Code Theory: i.e. Time Phase Theory a.k.a. Engineering Drafting Theory, 4 Distance Formula of 9 Planet, yield Hexagram Code to Moses Code then to Light Code. i.e. Metric system to Imperial system then to International Unit. These contributed to Engineering e.g. Telecommunication, Manufacturing.

Inheritance Decryption: There are Long generation, Wide generation interpolated to Orphanage generation, Broken generation and Ancient generation, which stick to inherited of father or mother gene. This constitute to the fundamental of medicine, called contagious disease.

Rocky Effect Decryption: There is a guarantee that mainstream will always remain constant, if there is guarantee victory; it has to uphold anything what confirmed and assured into equation of fighting. This constitute to the fundamental of manufacturing, called quality management.

Heaven Decryption: No more than 45 network. 3 network is coherent host. Each network has own translator as well as reflection. 18 same of a kind parallel network, 24 isolated series network. This constitute to the fundamental of social science, called mass media.

Continue on Next Page

4a. Published (Croyals Medicine Agency 石医医学署)

Quantum Treasure: The Three Biblical Treasure from Initial Christian Judification to Final Revelation Judgement, which is grace alone, many alternative way.
Economic Treasure: As above.
Christian Mathematics: Technology
War Insight: Weapon Methodology to Quantum Treasure
Criminology: Biblical Sins
Ending of Biblical Villain: Biblical Sinner Penalty
Hybrid Engineering: Military Technology

Christian Politics: Social Science
Social Engineering: Social Scamming
Christian Medicine: Genealogy Technology
Christian Finance: Economic Methodology to Quantum Treasure
Classification of Ethnic: Ethnic Labelling & Graded
Politics Evolution: Series to Economic Harvest Reinvention

Biblical Application: Doctrinal Training
Christian Education: Theology
Puritan Music: Church Music

Third World: The Utopia, defined by Stone Heritage Oriented. As this involved Trojan Horse, Word Prison, and Colony, correspond to Erotic Defect, Taste Defect, and Pollution Defect. Upside down of this is Oriental.
First World: The Renaissance, defined by Paper Heritage Oriented. As this involved Technology Frauding, Technology Hacking, Technology Scamming. Upside down of this is Promised Land.
Folks Revolution: The Cow Boy suit. White Supremacy. Pilgrim Heritage, Catholic Schism.
First of May Revolution: The Labour suit. Holistic Science, Fundamentalist Schism.
Thither Revolution: The Angel suit. Meta Correlation Schism, Puritan Schism.
Seal & Pirate: The Blueprint Decryption of Ancestry Heritage inheritor, Anointed Religion Duty.
Flagship & Imperial: The Blueprint Projection from Professional Technology Prestige, Specific Religion Prestige etc.
Signature & Testimonial: The Blueprint Cast out of Election Semitic Heritage and Ecumenical Church Anointed.
Official & Credential: Nativity & Meta. Possession of Authentic Inherit Blueprint. This begin with Migration/Exile of Major Prophet to Exile/Migration of Minor Prophet. i.e. Primary Atonement, Corner stone, and Redemption.
Meta Law: Directional, from top to down.

Dead Sequence: One major Schism and one minor schism and one diminished schism.

Continued

Utopia Beta: Industrial Revolution to Third World Manual Mode Engineering the Metrology Administration Products Fulfilment, a.k.a. Home Office Revolution. The Major Schism the 1st Dead Route. i.e. Democrats.
Promised Land: Industrial Revolution the 3rd, to Utopia Final Autopilot Mode Engineering the Robotic, a.k.a. Natalie Career Revolution i.e. Semitic Career. The Minor Schism the 2nd Dead Route. i.e. Nationalist.
Renaissance: Industrial Revolution the Final Pilot Mode Engineering the Simulation, to First World, a.k.a. Intellect Career Revolution i.e. Christian Career. The Diminished Schism the Fire Lake Route. i.e. Republican.
Oriental: Ecumenical Maturity Milestone yield the Industrial Revolution the Original, to Automatic Holistic Engineering Mode e.g. Infrastructure Cast Out. The Major Schism to Resurrection the 1st. i.e. Democracy.
Advent: Eschatology Events. Industrial Revolution the Greatest Time Lapsed, to Man Made Reinvented Engineering Mode e.g. Telecommunicational Medicine Projects. The Minor Schism to Resurrection the 2nd. i.e. Monarchy.

Footprint: Cast Out, Holoscopic the Axis of 3per
Foot-ink: Plotted, Aerial the Axis of 2per
Footage: Projection, Pentecostal the Axis of 1per

Sky App: Remote i.e. Client, Official & Legitimated Signature
Land Rover: Hostage i.e. Protocol, Certified & Tested Flagship
Sea Gate: Hosting i.e. Port, Opened & Operating Seal

Remaster: Cast Out, Orthogonal the Axis of 6per
Jeopardy: Plotted, Homogenous the Axis of 5per
Pilgrim: Projection, Holistic the Axis of 4per

Profit Ruler Grading: 7th, 6R, Marketplace, Commercialised
Margin Ruler Grading: 1st, 4R, Summit, Legitimated
Datum Ruler Grading: 6th, 3R, Dispatch, Publicised
Progressive Grading: Generic, 1R to 3R, Cluster, Cultivated

Latin Numbering: Generations
Roman Numbering: Series
Greek Numbering: Dimensional

Firefox: Landing
Netscape: Mapping
Explorer: Rolling
Errata 17Jan2023

Stellar: Universe Crystallisation, Organic Lambda #1-14

Sterilisation: Energy Crystallisation, Chemistry
Continued

Stellalisation: Social Crystallisation, Chemical

Artefact Boomerang: Quantum and Graded Schism merging is Lock 1 years, the 500 iteration.
Decorate Boomerang: Alternate to Extra Schism merging is Lock 10 years, the 5000 iteration.

Reynold: moles number X Constant= Meta Tither per Pi Number
Meta Scaled Boundary Footage, Property Value = Based on Reynold Number

Snow Train: Partial the Event Occurrence Rate
Transformer: Trinity the Intelligence Knowledge Value
Iron Man: Mono the Environment Hue Depth
Crabmachine: Multiple the Spiritual Nerve Power

Laboratory Estate: Headquarter the 11th
Tower Landscape: Less 1 Pillar

Errata 16/17/18/25/27Apr2020, 19/21/23May2020,
8/14/16/21/22/23/27/28Jun2020, 3/9/11/24/30Jul2020, 13Aug2020,
15Sep2020, 13Oct2020, 25/27/28Oct2020, 9/13/16Jan2021, 13Mar2021,
12Oct2022, 30Nov2022, 4Dec2022, 2Jan2023, 11Jan2023, 23Jan2023,
7Feb2023, 12Feb2023

Chinese Royal Flush™ Oriental Tonguepost 锄大地东方当铺

Caution: Some scam disguised Cult as Online Church. Prohibited worshiping Online Church, even with Covid-19 Epidemic, don't follow the trend, please take Spiritual carefully. No one can worship God without Tabernacle and without Fellowship.

"..You shall not take the name of the LORD your God in vain..." Exodus 20:1-17

Disclaimer: We are a Profit Organisation, rooted in Adelaide, Melbourne, Klang, Singapore, and Established in Johor Bahru. We very much like a Christian School as well as a Christian Solution Consultancy. We had accumulated certain extent of experiences & knowledge-base from Practical in Engineering, Politic, Music, Criminology, Theology, Economic, and Christian Education incl. Christian Mathematics, Christian Arts, Christian Science, Christian Music and Christian Law. We are serving upstream God Ministry and selectively downstream public ministry, e.g. Product Invention, Politic Revolution Campaign, Music Show, Crime Disruption Project, Theology Publication etc. You may find us in High Level teaching as close as Christian School by Christian Education Heritage. You may find us in High Level problem resolve as good as Christian Solution Consultancy in solving the real world Economic Science Development Issue. We are highly efficient, with nearly zero funding, we managed struggle to success, but with your devoted or little donation would shape us in many ways to sustain or speedy heading to victory against wicked power and evil network.

What we belief is Holistic the Hue Made of King. And this is in-regardless of Pollution
but purely Imagination of Schism of Hue. And for anyone has this Schism in Gross has
the Hue, and this is Freedom and Freedom. The Dream a little Dream and become Real
Value in the Cloud one day. Called Adventist i.e. "I Want This".

Precaution of Misconduction of Manual Adjustment or Judgemental e.g. Lawmaker for
Legislation, not about Opportunity but Risk Escalating, and this make Hue into Rainbow
6. Instead of that, promote of Humanity Weapon Treaty is the Biblical Way for Differ the
Salvation i.e. Permittable Max 10% Tither. Anything greater than this and momentum
consider Holysee of Highest Majesty.

Imprint of any Spiritual is Extra Mistake and more Mistake, and Yield no boosted Beneficial.

The Telecommunication Fouls, in Humanity Crime and War Crime, in Production of
Biscuit and Carbon Bill for Blocked Vulnerable Channel for Hygience Allergy as Prime.
*Chinese Literacy please translate from English which is the Whole Book Pillar.

Errata 28Jan2023

你的后裔和女人的后裔也彼此为仇，女人的后裔要伤你的头，你要伤他的脚跟 创世纪 3:15
Serpent Meta is Clock Wise. Eve Meta is Sarah the Egyptian Queen the Pharisee.

- <u>About Croyalflush Ministry Foundation, 关于活石事工基金会</u>

A. Our Vision:

Preserved Scientific Theology. i.e. Building the **Religion Unity Pillar**.

B. Our Mission:

Economic Science Research to Exit Federalism the Ecosystem Economic. i.e. **Salvation to whole Chinese Ultimately**.

C. Our Job:

Promote Long Hierarchy Company & Revealed as well as Opposed all kind of Christian Persecutions. i.e. **Advent of God Kingdom Decryption**.

D. Our Ministry:

Guideline to Disruption Climate Change Conspiracy. i.e. **Advanced Civilisation Threshold**.

E. Our Organisation & Milestone:

E1. Christian Education Aggregate
Published 'Fundamental of Christianity' website for Evangelism to Non believer and Reformation for Reborn Christian by Christian Science.

E2. Theology Aggregate
Published 'Matthew Gospel Commentary', 'New Theology Application' , 'Six Bible Myth', 'Nine Portion of Theology' Articles.

E3. Criminology Aggregate
Published 'End World Backup Plan' Book content incl. Crime Syndicate Network Revealed & Christian Persecution Revealed & Crime Conspirator Disruption Guide.

E4. Economic Aggregate
Published 'Light Encyclopedia™', Book total 700 Pages, content incl. Culture Heritage, Religion, Applied Physics, Social Science to Economic Science.

E5. Music Aggregate
Published CroyalPiano™ Music Encyclopedia, variety of Arrangement and Composed Music & Song. incl. Chinese Classic, Korean Pop, Piano Theme, Hymn Retro.

E6. Politic Aggregate
Published 'Editorial Articles' of each Country issue as well as Global Issue, to reach Ministry Agenda.

E7. Engineering Aggregate
Published CroyalDesign™ Machine Gallery incl. Cleared Leading Design & Manufacture Milestone for making Travel Gadget Grade Mobile Phone, Kitchen Appliance Grade P.O.S. Computer and Business Instrument Grade Meter.

F. Join Us

We are just small scale Educator & Consultancy Organisation, to survive we ought to grow up to moderate organisation for gaining power and influences. There are many phase and way you can join. If you saw this notice and feel interested please don't hesitate contact the Croyalflush Ministry Foundation's Secretary for delivering your interest, and there are alot of new jobs can be assigned.

Those Organization or Individuals who had partnership or contributes, this is the remembrance. We much care for any mis-leading or fallibility of Religion Belief, if yes, please let us know before you make report and take necessary action against us. Thank you!

The harvest is plentiful but the workers are few. Matthew 9:37
收割的工作多，而工人少。马太福音 9:37

About Founders 关于创办人

There is nothing but guide, please use at your own risk. The one who failure in life is the one who followed. Trust your heart.
这是专业的参考手册，滥用后果自负。人生失败者往往都是跟随者。要忠于自己的感觉。

- <u>About Founders 关于创办人</u>

Personal Miles Stone

On the dark side called myself God Father or Underground Theologian, has multiple Criminal Minority, incl. stealth, fraud, fighting, hardcore, gambling and hacking. Deliverance from acute surgery, fatal car accident, stage dismissal, job dismissal, tinnitus, temporary disable, marriage mistake, marriage failure to social blacklisting, a life regret to my ex-girlfriend, in which constituted the reason of writing **Foundation – of End World Backup Plan**, for Crime Syndicate Key Person Disruption.

Aspired in Mechanical Engineering, successfully graduated in Australia Top Tier University regretful defer 1½ year, Coupe with over 12 years Design Engineering skills in R&D Firm Since 2003' Portfolio with over 12 type of **Pillar – CroyalDesign of Machine Gallery**, retired at Forty years old amid apologetic to my Parents. Looking to startup Micro Retail Business as Making a Living for 2nd Part of Career Journey.

Thanks to Wikipedia.com, then founded **"Platform – Light Encyclopedia"** from 2013'-Present, a Light weighted but Comprehensive Encyclopedia (total 700 pages). Hence of the Manual Book, founded Non-profit organization Croyalflush Ministry Foundation Since 2011', progressively building Spiritually Diplomacy Ministry against Villain of Christianity, Rival of Christianity & Cult of Christianity.

On top of that, since childhood has cultured music skills, and then accumulated vast amount of on stage performing experiences in Chinese Orchestra, Folk Music Cafe, and Church Worship Ministry. Impromptu recording include over 21 type of Music Genre published as **"Legacy – CroyalPiano™ Music Encyclopedia"**.

Credit to Reformed Church and Fundamentalist Church, was trained as an Apostolic writer for Advanced Theology, Biblical Application to Global Ministry, Author of **"Croyalflush – Fundamental of Christianity"** for Christianity evangelism and reformation website since 2017'.

The Founders included My Parents, Father and Mother, in which involved in Legacy in terms of Inspiration on many topics in this books.

个人里程碑

在黑暗面自称为教父或地下神学家，有多个小型犯罪记录，包括偷窃，欺诈，打架，嫖妓，赌博和骇客。从急性手术、致命车祸、舞台解雇、职场解雇、耳鸣、暂时残废、婚姻错误、婚姻失败到社会黑名单被释放，对前女友来说是一生的遗憾，因此构成了撰写《世界末日备份计划-基础》的原因，即犯罪集团关键人物揭破。

渴望修读机械工程，并成功毕业于澳大利亚顶级大学，遗憾推迟一年半毕业，自2003年以来拥有超过十二年在研发公司的设计工程技能，累计荣获超过十二种设计产品奖项里程碑。收录在《石医设计机器画廊-梁柱》，四十岁退休的我对父母道歉。展望于我的微商零售生意当作后半生的职场生涯。

感谢 WIKIPEDIA.COM，从2013年至今创立了《活石光百科全书-平台》，轻量但全方位综合百科全书（共七百页）。因这本秘笈书，成立了活石事工基金会始于二零一一年，渐进的与基督教的反派，基督教的对手，基督教的邪派，建立属灵外交事工。

除此之外，从小学习音乐，并在华乐团、民间音乐咖啡馆和教会崇拜事工积累了大量的舞台演出经验。即兴录音包括超过二十一种类型的音乐曲风，《石医钢琴音乐百科-遗产》。

归功于归正派教会和原教旨主义派教会的培训成为使徒作家，专长于高级神学与全球事工圣经的应用等，自2017年，创立了基督教福音派和归正网站，《活石基督教-概论》。

创办人包括我的父母，爸爸和妈妈，参与献出思想启发遗产包括其中在书本出现的多个标题。

Made in the USA
Columbia, SC
19 May 2024

34857494R00107